Just *One* Suitcase?!

Just *One* Suitcase?!

(Escaping Winter)

A. Margaret Caza

Shoreline

Shoreline, 23 Ste. Anne
Sainte-Anne-de-Bellevue, Quebec H9X 1L1
shorelinepress@bell.net · 514-457-5733 · shorelinepress.ca

Legal deposit: Library and Archives Canada
Bibiothèeque et Archives nationales du Quéebec

Library and Archives Canada Cataloguing in Publication
Caza, A. Margaret
Just *one* suitcase?! : escaping winter /
A. Margaret Caza.

ISBN 978-1-896754-93-2
1. Caza, A. Margaret-Travel-Europe-Humor.
2. Caza, A. Margaret-Travel-Florida-Juno Beach-Humor.
3. Caza, A. Margaret-Family-Humor. 4. Europe-
Description and travel-Humor. 5. Juno Beach (Fla.)-
Description and travel-Humor. I. Title.

D922.C39 2011   914.04'556   C2011-902537-X

To Renaud -
Ahhh, the fun times we had....

CONTENTS

INTRODUCTION

Escaping winter was not the first thing on my mind when I was 8 years old, living in Campbellton, New Brunswick, and having enormous fun tobogganing, skiing, skating and building snow forts with my brother, Bud. Under the watchful gaze of the Sugarloaf Mountain, winter was delicious! Why would anyone want to get away from glorious snow and ice?!

Ten years later, in 1948, life was still fun. My family moved to the province of Québec, I graduated from business college, found a satisfying job, and winter was still pretty much okay.

Tacking on a bunch more years, however, and the snowball effect went into overdrive. Winter had to be dealt with.

Those years included marriage and children, as well as planning, organization and hard work to get our construction and farm equipment business rolling. My husband, Renaud, did the hard work. I quit my job, stayed at home, had babies and created havoc with endless projects.

Back in the old days, 1952 in my case, when the romantic ballad 'You Belong to Me' (Fly the ocean in a silver plane...) meant plodding across the sky in an old converted-to-cargo B-52 bomber to work in the Arctic, I didn't dream that 50-odd years later I'd be travelling much faster across that same sky in the company of laid-back travel groups, with the advantage of professional organization and guidance.

While my travels as a single involved the usual last-minute decisions, mix-ups of accommodations, misunderstandings, and a strong but unwarranted trust in timetables, once the jolly circumstance of two cultures, two languages, two sexes and, occasionally, three generations were added, what emerged from our misadventures proved that planned travel, like planned parenthood, although undoubtedly much neater, is not necessarily more exciting or rewarding.

In fact, it might help today's traveller to realize that, hair-raising as travel boo-boos might be at the moment of commission, later – much later – all those maddening little travel dramas will be remembered without rancor. In fact, they'll be dragged out and celebrated. They'll be polished up whenever and wherever there's an audience and, trust me, they will emerge burnished to a soft patina of good times, fondly remembered.

So, that's why this book is just a quirky look at how our family travels unravelled. It's about the misadventures of this quixotic family tilting at the windmills of conventional travel, and ending up not sadder, perhaps only slightly wiser, but altogether infinitely richer in spirit in a world often improved by a flair for the untimely.

I
THE WAY IT WAS

Of All Places, Greenland

In the darkness of early morning my mother and I were in a horse-and-buggy taxi going along our gravel street to the train station. There, Mr. Gilker, a family friend, took over for my mother, who was scheduled for surgery. He accompanied me on the Ocean Limited from Campbellton, New Brunswick, on the Restigouche River, to Sussex, where my grandparents owned and operated a small bakery. My older brother, Bud, was in school so had to stay in the care of a part-time sitter after school and our father after work.

At the station our plywood suitcases, heavy even before packing, were loaded onto iron-wheeled trolleys to take them to the baggage car.

Our railroad car smelled of oranges and the unforgettable train-smell of dusty-smoky green velour that cushioned the varnished wooden bench-seats. There was a pot-bellied stove, a small woodpile and a scuttle full of coal. Flickering gas lamps shuddered with the clanking rumble of the train's rocking motion. It was October and late at night when we arrived in Sussex. My grandparents, Agnes and Linus, were waiting at the station. Mr. Gilker claimed our luggage and we all walked across the street to enter the door that led to my grandparents' upstairs apartment above the bakery. It was 1935. I was 5 years old and this was my first travel experience.

In 1939, World War II broke out. In 1942 my father, a Stationary Engineer, joined the army and after basic training went with his regiment to Europe, where he served in the Canadian army for 3 years. These soldiers had travelled from all parts of Canada via train to Halifax where they boarded ships that transported them overseas with their great canvas kit bags and heavy canvas haversacks.

I remember once a week my mother packed a box to send to him overseas. The box sat on a small table in the dining room, and it was an adventure for Bud and me to find unique little extras to tuck in amongst the ordinary homey supplies.

The war ended on Sept. 2nd, 1945. V-J Day.

After returning to his peace-time job with Gray's Creamery, our father decided in 1948 to rejoin the army, accepting a posting in Montreal. Our family travelled there by train.

Bud also joined the army, I went to business college, graduating in 1950, and found a job in the engineering department of Canadian Arsenals. It was there I met Renaud Caza, a young French-Canadian Civil Engineer. In 1951, I bought the first vehicle our family ever owned, a second-hand Mercury, vintage 1945.

A year later, motivation for more travel struck when the cultural, religious and language differences between the handsome Frenchman from St. Anicet and me prompted me to give up my job and go to work as a secretary for the U.S.A.F. in, of all places, Greenland, to think over this important relationship.

Renaud drove me to the military section of the Montreal airport, put a diamond ring on my finger (for protection, he said), and we had a last hug.

I waved goodbye to Renaud and climbed aboard my first ever airplane. The seating in our converted-to-cargo B-52 bomber was a canvas-webbing bench along the port side of the plane's interior, facing bolted-down crates and equipment. All the passengers (except me) wore military fatigues. We all wore parachute harnesses.

After landing at Goose Bay, Labrador, to pick up additional freight and passengers, we were told we had to wait until the only approach to our Greenland landing strip – which had been blocked by a giant iceberg – was accessible and no longer socked in by weather. I was given a bed in the women's barracks, where I slept for two nights in my slacks and sweater (no carry-on bag). On the third day, we were cleared to depart. Next stop, Greenland.

Later I was invited to the flight deck to observe the approach to Greenland. I had several minutes to view the vast, mountainous, treeless, snow-covered expanse of my new habitat, bathed in a brilliant red-gold sunset.

I was back on my canvas-webbing bench hanging onto my harness and seat belt as, with wing tip swooping perilously close to bare rock wall, we plunged steeply into the 50-mile-long-canyon corridor of the Tunugdliarfik Fjord toward the runway approach – and landed.

My new home was a small, broad-based pocket set into the vastness of Greenland's 10,000-foot-thick, 700,000-square-mile ice cap.

My first impression of Greenland, after the showy sunset and the tight approach between mountains, was that if you want to get away from it all to think things over, you couldn't get much more remote than Greenland. Next was acknowledgment of a military setting of Quonset huts, barracks, mess halls, snack bar, Service Club, Post Exchange, and other low-slung, gray-painted military-type architecture huddled in the blue shadows of treeless slate-gray mountains.

The monotone blue-gray colour of everything was startling. Runway and road blended with harsh gray rock, blue buses, blue-clad airmen, blue jeeps, pale, blue-tinged banks of snow. Melting snow sent swirls of steam spiralling upward from the short stretch of paved road, and I breathed invigorating draughts of the incredibly clean, pure air, untainted by industry, chilled and freshly blown off the glacier.

After meeting Matron in the Women's Barracks in the Hospital Compound, I was shown the communal washroom with its row of toilet stalls, rows of sinks and two galvanized metal showers, then directed to my small room, which had a wardrobe cupboard, a bureau, a desk and a high, hospital-type bed. A bare bulb dangled from the middle of the ceiling. Folded sheets, a blanket and a pillow rested on the thin, striped mattress. A window looked out at a high mountain face, down which tumbled a thin cascade of water.

Next was introduction to the mess hall. I followed my clattering, laughing barracks mates down a series of long low corridors that branched out to lead to various buildings, connected to each other by more corridors. This was the hospital complex, which could operate like a little village in impossibly heavy weather.

The next morning the procedure of "clearing the base" was explained to me, and I was assigned my job in Air Installations, Engineering.

I soon found that living in a 3 by ¾-mile valley of granite, gravel and permafrost, on the edge of a glacier, with a male/female ratio of 3,000 to 40, took a bit of getting used to.

The short summer arrived suddenly, bringing tiny flowers poking through patches of scrubgrass and around coarse hills of gravel. Delicate scraps of blue, yellow and pink, braced up by wisps of leaves, peeked determinedly from inhospitable rock crevasses.

Hiking brought other visual treats: an eagle peered down from its eyrie, ravens swooping, clumps of bracken clutching desperately just above the ice of the fjord, high ridges of gray, white and black rock standing out, sharply etched against a summertime sky that covered the canyon like a flat sheet of blue Bristol board.

High summer came, and I watched the sun bobbing along the horizon, ducking behind mountaintops and out the other side without really setting, so that for the space of a few short weeks, night was nothing more than a dullish afternoon edged by bright blue twilight - and a wonderful opportunity to mountain climb at night. In daylight!

At midnight, I climbed a mountain overlooking the harbour, appreciating the eerie navy blue and gold shadows cast over the distant glacier, and looked down at the base as it lay, stern and military, even in slumber: a ghost town scene of night without darkness. Not much different from the daytime view, but without the grace of humanity. No movement lurked in the quiet, shaded windows, no vehicle trundled patiently down the vacant road at the 20-miles-per-hour speed limit, no raven swooped purposefully toward half-hidden prey and no aircraft droned overhead. A perfect, noiseless calm.

Mountain climbing was a favourite summer activity and it was not unusual to see one or more loops of roped-together climbers, dressed in bright reds, blues, yellows, and oranges, festooned across the rock face of the southern range like strings of brightly coloured beads decorating the stern bracken-clad bosoms of the surrounding mountains.

Summer brought Greenland's most spectacular feature: icebergs. Released by summer's heat with earth-shaking violence, glaciers, fanning out from Greenland's ice cap, expelled massive icebergs from their prison of thousands of years. White around the edges, with jagged hard cores of brilliant, translucent blue, these paleocrystic icebergs strutted down the silvery green melt-waters of the Fjord, past the harbour, sometimes stalling long enough at the end of the runway that they blocked incoming air traffic, and had to be dynamited or roped and towed out of the way.

Scattered over the northern range flanking the glacier, mountain goats and musk ox, followed closely by their delicate, white fleeced kids, strolled calmly along craggy peaks, and tiptoed down narrow ledges, attentive in their pursuit of bits of tough grasses.

Along the trails, bleached bones and animal skulls lay on the sand, where they might have been for centuries. Adding to the desolation of the view were large, tangled bundles of hair shed by Greenland's animals after the harsh winters. Pushed by brisk winds these rough tangles of hair rolled down mountainsides and skittered across the deserted sand flats and runway like tumbleweed across an arid desert.

Then, almost suddenly, the brief summer merged with an autumn scarcely seen except as brilliant foliage hugging close to the surrounding mountains, as advancing darkness combined with fine mists and dense fogs, heralding winter.

Even in winter, there were contradictions of climate and Narsarsuaq, snuggled into its small stretch of valley, experienced the phenomenon of the wind coasting downhill off the mountains, warming by compression by 4 degrees Fahrenheit per 1000 feet of descent, creating incredible foens (Chinooks) in the dead of winter.

In all seasons, Greenland's gale force winds were the reason stout cables were attached to the women's barracks entrance, to serve as a guide, and something to grab hold of as we scrambled off the buses after work and struggled hand-over-hand to gain the barracks door without being blown off our feet.

In mid-summer, I joined a small group of co-workers to climb up Hospital Hill and hike back to our very accessible glacier. In the distance, across a rock and scrub meadow, it came into view. Tucked tightly between the canyon walls like instantly frozen white water – a giant swath of white cutting through grey rock. Here the mountainsides on either side of the glacier as we approached, instead of being slate-like and jagged, had the smooth appearance of being loosely folded. Stretching as far as eye could see, sandpapered by ice, storms and winds of countless centuries, they rolled and unrolled into the distance.

We hurried ahead determinedly because, in addition to the unaccustomed heat, we swatted at hungry black flies, feeling more miserable, sweaty and itchy by the minute. Mosquitoes added their sting, too, as they swarmed over the damp, spongy permafrost hillside and us. Hanging over us, and following us in black pepper-looking clouds, they rushed into nostrils and mouths along with the air we breathed. Hastily, we touched boot-toe to glacier then retreated. It would take more than the sudden disappearance of the insects as we arrived at the crest of Hospital Hill to erase the ravages of their attentions.

Down the remaining length of trail in line with the hospital compound we made our sorry and dejected way, and when we reached the women's barracks, our group separated. Waving dispirited good-byes, I trailed into the building, through the long grey corridors, back to my quarters and, grabbing a towel and a handful of fresh clothes, made a beeline for the barracks washroom. In no time, I was ensconced in the battered grey galvanized shower stall with its cheap plastic curtain, appreciatively letting cool, refreshing water run over me until I was reasonably certain I would not expire of terminal sweat and black flies.

There was no doubt about Greenland's being a challenging place right from the start, but black flies? Ah, now *there* was a challenge!

∞∞∞∞

It was overcast and windy when a group of us boarded an icebreaker to visit an Eskimo village northwest of the base.

Arriving at our destination, we could clearly see there was a docking problem. Our boat deck was high above the low-lying bank, plus we couldn't get close enough to butt into it. However, the crew seemed to be familiar with this circumstance and two Eskimo men approached, reaching for rope lines to position our boat and secure our gangplank.

This was no sturdy, adjustable steel gangplank with helpful side rails. What we had to help us gain land turned out to be an unreinforced board about 10 inches wide placed across the 8-foot wide downhill gap between deck and shore. Checking the distance between the plank and what lay beneath it, I looked dizzily at chunks of glacial ice sloshing in the freezing, dark water some 10 feet below. I riveted my gaze on the opposite end of the plank and, following the others, teetered unsteadily across, only then realizing that I would later have to walk the same plank, uphill, to regain the boat deck.

While there, we explored the village, visiting a small cemetery, a schoolhouse, drying racks of fish, and the ruins of a burned church.

The sheer loneliness of this simple, quiet place with its sparse scattering of tidy square homes gave credence to the old saw: "An interesting place to visit but I wouldn't want to live there," and made our rough barracks, with all its stern amenities, seem downright luxurious.

When we were safely back on board the icebreaker, the men pulled in the plank, drew in the line tossed to them by an Eskimo standing on shore, and we waved and cheered as our icebreaker moved away from the settlement and chugged back toward the base.

Darkness was almost on us in the shortened autumn day. Hungry and cold, we made our way port-side to the warm galley where frying hot dogs, hamburgers and onions crackled deliciously and the savoury aroma of strong, black coffee filled the frost-tinged air.

∞∞∞∞∞

Greenland also offered the unique perspective of special occasions celebrated far from home, with the curious ability of remote places and circumstances to bring strangers together in friendship.

Even birthdays were different in such a setting and one day, I cadged the necessary ingredients and use of an oven from a Mess Sergeant to make a birthday cake for one of the airmen in the office.

Ah, what an occasion. Half a dozen airmen in fatigues and several civilian engineers gathered in a dim corner of the engineering storeroom around a fresh pot of hot coffee from the Mess Hall. A giant, crudely painted cardboard HAPPY BIRTHDAY card hung suspended over a small table holding a delicate coconut cake atop which a single utility candle glowed – and there, in the midst of Greenland's rugged isolation, far from hearth, home and civilization, ten lusty voices and one treble rose raucously from an open window of the Air Installations storage room, and "For he's a Jolly Good Felll-ooo-www...." reverberated up the canyon walls and rang clearly in the still, cold air.

As autumn merged with winter, it brought the incredible brilliance of stars clinging in thick masses, standing out brightly against the background of the intensely black night sky, with no surrounding ground illumination to dilute their clarity.

A favourite pastime on such nights was to stand outside and watch - and listen to – the dramatic crackle and zing-like static of brilliant green Northern Lights as they zipped, pounced and changed patterns, like translucent satin, shot with rose, gold and violet, rippling languidly across the arctic sky.

Then, darkness would set in as inevitable clouds lowered down over the mountaintops, a mantle of thick, gray fog rolled in from the Tunugdliarfik Fjord, and winter slithered into place, bringing a tangible gloom to our isolated little sunless valley. A feeling of unreality took hold, almost like being in a science fiction drama: We were in a high-walled box with no way out, and the lid slowly lowering.

Greenland - an outstanding place to visit – but choose your season.

All Roads Lead to Florida

There's no doubt that marriage changes travel. In 1952, when I married Renaud, the man I had gone to Greenland to make up my mind about, I felt I'd had enough travel.

I had wrestled with the possible dire consequences of a bicultural union, and now that that was resolved, all I wanted was for us to go to a quiet place and live happily ever after. At least that's what I thought I wanted.

But we couldn't *not* have a honeymoon, could we? Of course not. Two weeks after I left Greenland, we were married and embarking on a New York City honeymoon. Honeymoon? Well, I wonder what knot-head dreamed up the idea that two totally different people (man/woman, what could be more different?) should risk everything right at the outset of a young relationship by travelling somewhere on a wedding trip. "They'll get to know each other," is a reckless premise, because if ever two people should not be thrown together intimately in a travel situation, it's just after they've tied the knot.

As a matter of fact, if I remember correctly, Renaud and I had our first disagreement en route to New York City, 500 miles after we said, "I do." Although it was a gentle discord (something about how he didn't believe in road maps and we were lost), it opened my eyes, and undoubtedly his, too, to the realization that we had each just promised to take an almost total stranger until death do us part.

We settled on stopping early at a motel for the night, finding our directions the next morning at breakfast, and continuing to our destination through the day's golden autumn brilliance. It was November.

22

As soon as we breezed into New York City, we booked on a sightseeing bus that immediately had a flat tire. A replacement bus arrived and took us to the Empire State Building, where we zipped up to the observation deck, and were properly awed.

Back in our own car at the end of the afternoon, we bumper-hugged through endless traffic, ricocheted off Long Island on a wrong turn off the rush-hour thruway, and in the midst of blaring horns and endless lanes of traffic, Renaud said, "I've had enough of this madhouse traffic. I want to go home."

Romantically, I hoped that the honeymoon had been reduced to a thrilling 2½ days of wedded bliss on wheels because Renaud could hardly wait for us to get settled into our new, cozy 4-room rented bungalow in Nitro (an explosives industry village) so we could be delightfully, privately alone together to work on our charming differences.

I endorsed his sentiments. I, too, wanted to go home. What I couldn't even have imagined, as we headed straight back toward the Canadian border, was that, "I want to go home," might become our ever-after holiday theme song.

Whether it was passion or geography that urged us homeward then, it doesn't really matter. What matters is that we learned nothing from the experience, because one year later, in November of 1953, heedlessly, we quit our jobs, bought a homemade red plywood trailer from a business acquaintance, gave up the lease on our rented house, sold some of our secondhand furniture, stored the rest and went to Florida on a first anniversary holiday. The stored furniture, our clothes, our secondhand 1947 gray Pontiac, and the little red plywood trailer were all we owned in the world as we embarked on this impractical, free-spirited dash to our warm destination.

Of course, we didn't know the first thing about towing a trailer, or about living in a 6-by-8-foot space with a newly acquired life partner. But it was wonderful! We were young, fearless and in love. It's a good thing that we were also agile, and fairly bump-proof because "Little Red" was only 5 feet tall (we were both taller), and curved down to a point at the rear. The interior walls were varnished plywood and I made red and white gingham curtains for the windows.

It looked very campy. It smelled rather campy, too, but that was okay. Since it was so small, there was little house-keeping to be done – except for the floor, which had to be swept on hands and knees with a whiskbroom. There was no refrigerator and we cooked on a 2-burner Coleman camp stove. There was no bathroom either, but that was provided by gas stations that would let us park overnight or by trailer parks and campgrounds where we could book in and even get showers,and use laundry facilities.

Young and unencumbered as we were then, two months of life in a trailer too short to stand up in proved hard on the nerves for both of us. By the time we arrived back in Montreal, in a December blizzard, we were broke, jobless and homeless, with two bushels of oranges in mesh bags on the back seat. We were fed up with Florida, trailer life and, at least a little bit, with each other. We have since looked back fondly to those red teardrop trailer days, which proved to be the training wheels to future vacation destinations.

Within days of arriving back in Canada in a heavy snowstorm, we rented a small studio apartment in the heart of Montreal and found work – I with *Readers' Digest*, Renaud with a heavy-equipment company.

The irresponsible adventure was over. We settled gladly into our new roles, waited for spring, and did no more travelling until 8 years, 3 kids, a couple of dogs, a cat, a hamster, and a burgeoning construction and agricultural equipment business later.

Most people who want to escape winter seek out a variety of destinations. They want new vistas, to experience the world. However, 'All roads lead to Rome' didn't exactly apply to us. It soon became abundantly clear that, although we wanted to experience new lands and cultures, we had neither the stamina nor the budget to take advantage of all that the world had to offer. We were not typical, well-heeled tourists, out to examine and appreciate the world. We were escapists, burdened with debt, who had no choice but to do our escaping using only available cash (no credit), and a fortunate sense of humour.

Several Florida vacations down the road, we knew pretty well what to expect. That didn't deter us, and every so often, we'd get the 'escape' bug again and look around for some place new to sample. Somewhere a bit more exotic, perhaps, and sure enough, well before our schedule indicated (sometimes before the bags were unpacked, and once, before they were even unloaded from the plane). Renaud forgot that he was there to relax and have a good time, and became as lonely (for Florida), as a homesick 8-year-old at summer camp for the first time.

What was missing became apparent to me very early. People. Family. Extended family. Renaud missed the business, where he was virtually surrounded by friends and relatives of the community he had lived in all his life. It was easy to see why we kept boomeranging back to Florida. Florida, where French appears to be almost the third language, next to English and Spanish, was where our St. Anicet friends and family went in winter. So long as we were in Florida, we were quite literally at home visiting, playing cards, bike riding, swimming, and partying – just like in St. Anicet. The only difference was Florida had palm trees and sand instead of icicles and snow.

The venue in the early days was Vito's: an affordable, down-at-the-heels oceanside motel in Juno Beach, just north of West Palm Beach, where we set down vacation roots in the mid-'60s that dug deeper every year.

I'm not complaining. It was pleasant there, lacking in amenities perhaps, but comfortable. Like an old shoe – a very old shoe, with scruffy toes, runover heels and broken laces.

Sitting on the worn boards shoring up a sandy bluff overlooking the Atlantic Ocean, idly watching the Florida sun put on its engaging dawn performance, was balm for the soul. Not a splurge of glitter and luxury, but panacea for the vagaries of work and weather left behind in winterbound Québec.

Not that we didn't appreciate other countries. Over time we did go and we did see the beauty of other lands. We experienced other cultures, museums, restaurants. We enjoyed casual conversations with the people who lived there. We bought tourism directories and adjusted to jet lag. Still, our vacation time was short and when conditions didn't cooperate: "I'd rather be in Florida," Renaud would say glumly, glowering at the overcast skies of purportedly sunny Spain, the bustling straw market in Nassau, the crowded streets of downtown London in a heavy drizzle, the stifling heat of Cozumel, the indifferent hotel staff in Jamaica, the dazzling sights and sounds of Las Vegas, the insane traffic of Acapulco. After a summer of 16+ hour work days, this was not the best way for him to unwind and recharge his batteries.

Still, if this was the only way to savour a wisp of foreign lands -- by bumping into them briefly as we caromed wildly toward Florida -- then so be it. The big difference this made toward our attitude about travel is that later, we didn't plan excitedly for the foreign adventures ahead when Renaud had that far-away look in his eyes while telling me about friends returning from Italy.

When he optimistically suggested, "Let's go there for our next holiday," I knew better than to drop everything and whisk over to the bookstore for an Italian phrase book. 'Bonjourno' and 'Arrivederci' would be enough because, in short order, we were going to end up in Florida anyway. Just like what happened with Mexico.

Don't Drink the Water

By the mid-1960s, Florida was firmly imbedded as a sunny benchmark when we needed to get away from the demands of business and winter. It was far from our responsibilities, and it was affordable – if we didn't aim too high.

Then, one day, Mexico appeared on the horizon. Enthusiastic friends (staunch fans of Mexico) persuaded us that Acapulco was paradise. They said we didn't know what we were missing.

Within minutes, Renaud surprised us both by saying, "Let's go."

At the same time, he surfaced with the notion that organized tours were not for us. He said, "I hear that the only way to see the real Mexico is to go on our own." No organized tours or well-researched itineraries for us. It sounded like a good idea.

First thing the next morning I called a travel agent, who agreed that we couldn't go wrong with colourful Mexico, and booked a flight. To Acapulco.

Thus were we launched on what became a country-by-country learning experience that uncovered the fact that what we really wanted was the brightness, gaiety and music suggested by picture postcards and travel brochures of exotic places. We hadn't given any thought to the possibility of away-from-home realities such as unfamiliar food, unyielding beds, too yielding plumbing, foreign currencies, and diarrhea.

Back in 1965, there was nothing exotic about landing in Acapulco at midnight with no reservations. At the airport, we stood near the arrivals exit looking perplexed. Within minutes, a taxi driver sidled over and offered to take us in tow. We accepted.

Racing away from the airport in his dilapidated little two-door Morris, we zoomed around a curve. Ahead of us in the darkness, a man and woman struggled out of the bushes, into the beam of our headlights, fighting their way across the road.

Facing our approaching car, the woman gained freedom. She held her arms toward our sweep of headlights beseechingly, but the man grabbed her and pulled her back. Renaud and I clung tightly to each other as our driver, laughing maniacally, leaned into the wheel and, astonishingly, picked up speed as he aimed right at them, swerving only at the last moment. We glanced back through the rear window. There was nothing but blackness and silence.

At that moment, Renaud, who had insisted earlier that he didn't want to be a tourist but wanted to soak up local colour, would have given his eye teeth to be cosily installed in a thoroughly Americanized hotel. And so would I. But it was too late for that.

We were in Acapulco less than an hour, and had already soaked up sufficient local colour. A faint, familiar hum rumbled near my left ear. I knew it was Renaud. And I knew what he was thinking. And I thought so too. We were inexperienced tourists from little St. Anicet, hurling through the dark night in a vaguely threatening situation.

After a while, our driver pointed out clusters of lights in the distance to our left. He glanced back at us, leered, and said gruffly "Money, money, money, huh... Big hotels, hey? Ha ha ha...."

Nearing downtown Acapulco, Renaud gave the driver a slip of paper with the address of his nephew Jeannot, who was vacationing in Acapulco, thus launching us on an extended taxi tour of the back streets of town.

We didn't find Jeannot that night, but a lithe, black haired, heavy mustached man with a broad smile and bare feet materialized in front of us on a dead-end, pot-holed street of homes protected by bars and gates. He wore what looked like blue cotton pyjamas, and carried a scimitar that he swooshed back and forth, as he sauntered toward us.

The hum in my left ear revved up again, and I agreed silently that we were done for. But blue-pyjamas turned out to be a uniformed policeman on patrol and, after carrying on a friendly conversation with our driver, he waved us on our way.

Our driver then brought us to the El Cid Hotel, on the main drag and across the street from the beach, and we were led up to our room on the second floor.

It was two in the morning, we had just had an expensive and unproductive tour of the lesser parts of Acapulco and, Lord help us, a whole month of days in this unfamiliar place stretched ahead, with an unhappy husband humming like a jar of disconsolate bees.

Our room was large, air-conditioned, and had a window overlooking the street paralleling the beach. A bottle of water stood on the bathroom counter. We had a small drink from it, brushed our teeth, showered and went to bed.

In the morning, things looked brighter. Our hotel was comfortable, the weather magnificent. By the third day of total inactivity, we were as rested as we wanted to be.

There was nothing to do. We aren't beach people, especially when the beach is crowded and the water, instead of invitingly clear, cool and sparkling, washes sulkily over hot sand. We walked to the market place, and toured the Super-Super. Our outings were brief and aimless – nothing to do and nobody to visit.

One day, wandering down a side street, we found a sports arena. Everyone we asked assured Renaud there would be boxing at the sports arena mañana. There wasn't. Maybe they didn't understand the question. We took the trek daily, with the same scenario.

Every day after breakfast we hurried across the street from hotel to beach as vehicles with cracked windshields (the result of hastily applied brakes) charged wildly down the boulevard. One look at Acapulco traffic was all it took to convince us not to rent a car.

Then one day on the beach, we found Renaud's nephew and his pals, who were used to Mexico and Acapulco and found our naiveté amusing. They introduced us to wild downtown traffic in their rented jeep and showed us that at 10 p.m., the traffic lights were turned off and it was every man for himself.

The next morning, they drove us around hill country, where wild pigs scurried through the brush. "Who owns them?" asked Renaud. "Whoever catches them," said Jeannot. They took us to a bullfight (never again). The matador was killed by the bull, but at least he had a choice. The bull didn't have a choice. Another matador moved into the ring and did the job. The bull was in the ring to *be* killed.

Then, there was an astounding night club called La Huerta, a sort of supermarket style nightclub-brothel. We felt secure because Jeannot and his buddies were with us, but we were unprepared for the show. Music was louder than loud and dancers on the centrally-located stage were in revealing costumes. One in particular was a good 6 feet tall and beautiful, with long, straight black hair and high, high heels. We were both gawking. of course, and when the dance ended, the tall beauty stepped down off the stage, walked over to Renaud, took his head in her hands, turned it away from her, and pulled up his chin to shut his astonished mouth.

Somewhere in all this, I drank a Coco-Loco on the beach (with contaminated ice cubes) and ended up with the worst kind of revenge. Jeannot and friends came through sportingly with some chalky medication and the infuriating chuckles of those who have been through it and know that you are indeed suffering, but will survive. The next few days were a miserable blur.

We lasted 17 days, 2 gentle earthquakes, and a fire on the mountain that looked uncomfortably like lava (surely not). Then, one night, our air conditioner broke down and Renaud said, "I can't take any more of this, what do you say we call Vito?" (Our motel proprietor in Florida). I answered, eagerly, "Okay." At last, we would have English language newspapers and television and, above all, assurance that, beyond Acapulco's encircling mountains, the rest of the world existed.

∞∞∞∞

Breakfast the next morning was a festive occasion. We had purpose. Something to do. At noon, on the way to the downtown office of Eastern Airlines to see about early departure on our 30-day tickets, we discovered a Woolworth store where there was a lunch counter. American cooking, at last! We sat at the high counter. Renaud ordered a hamburger and a beer. I was very hungry, but still queasy from the revenge, so I ordered from a picture on the menu of a delicious looking, tall frosted milkshake. It turned out to be neither frosted nor delicious because it was made with evaporated milk, undiluted, unchilled, and served in a glass straight from the hot dishwasher. It was thick all right, but it would have taken a more desperate person than I to swallow it.

From there, we walked to Eastern Airline's office where their Mr. Diaz looked at us benevolently, shrugged, and said, "Whatever you want; wherever you want to go." Then, another walk to the telephone office where we stood in line to make a long distance call to Vito to tell him we would be at Palm Beach International the next day.

"I meet you at airport," Vito growled in his gravely mumble. "I try to fine you somethin', someplace to stay." And he did.

Ah, Florida! Cool sea breezes, swooping gulls and rustling palms painted the familiar Florida picture. We were installed in our motel unit at the top of the bluff, Renaud still sound asleep – a look of vast contentment etched softly on his face. He was where he wanted to be. Not that I wasn't, too, but it was still hard to believe we had done it again and that less than 24 hours earlier we had stood on the beach in Acapulco, watching a Pacific sunset, with 13 days remaining on our return tickets.

I carried my cup of coffee down to the beach and sat on the wooden plank-bench imbedded at the foot of the bluff. Gulls wheeled and screeched as I took another sip of barely warm coffee, pushed my toes deeper into the cool, damp sand and tightened the belt of my pink striped cotton housecoat. Our travel about-faces were becoming as traditional as the wheeling gulls – but with a predictable destination. Well, there are all kinds of travellers: The ones who want to see foreign shores and those who really just need to get away from their everyday work world – and escape winter.

∞∞∞∞

We did not visit Mexico again until 20 years later - in 1985. On a cruise ship.

We learned that cruises are not cancelled on account of hurricanes. That's what we headed into upon leaving Florida's Port Everglades. Why would they cancel a sailing, with all its attendant arrangements? The show must go on.

This was interesting in several respects. We were travelling with friends Mendo and Georgette and, although seasickness took precedence for the first few hours, the real challenge was maintaining our balance as we investigated the ship. Afternoon activities were sparsely attended and at that evening's show the stage's curtains whipped back and forth and the audience was delivered an impromptu main event as performers fought to keep their balance. It was on this cruise that we observed first-hand just how flexible ships are. Leaving the bow of the ship to return from the Disco Lounge to our staterooms, we looked down the long length of narrow corridor with rails on either side to hang onto, and the floor of this corridor was undulating! Sort of like a crazy-walk in an amusement park.

By morning, the captain had opted for safe harbour and we settled, unscheduled but securely, in Key West.

Of course, while in Key West, we weren't about to miss the opportunity to visit the historical home of the great American author Ernest Hemingway, and meet the descendants of his cats.

Then, a hurricane induced, very chilly trolley ride of the town before returning to our ship, where we waited out the storm before continuing to our Mexican destination, Cancun. Cancun and Cozumel provided sunshine, less fierce winds and a bus tour that took us to Chitzen Itza, where it was beyond hot and humid.

We thought it would be a good idea to climb a pyramid, but a close-up view of the height of the stone blocks, the sight of climbers and descenders hanging onto ropes and rusted chains to achieve their destination, combined with the extreme heat and humidity dissuaded us.

The Temple of Kukulkan (El Castillo) looked like a good prospect, but time constraints plus the heat led us to try what we thought would be an easier climb up through a tunnel from the base to the top. It wasn't easier because the

Maya are short in stature so the tunnel was low-ceilinged. It was also humid and very earthy. We had to crouch through the tunnel. With such a tight pathway, it didn't take long for claustrophobia to set in and we turned back, squeezing past the climbing crowd to reach daylight.

The Maya were learned in mathematics, astronomy and architecture so there was much to see and marvel at, leaving tourists to wonder why, with all this intelligence, was human sacrifice so prevalent. Our tour included a pit where, in ancient times, sacrifices were made. Victims were thrown off, or forced to jump off the cliffs into the water at the bottom of the pit – and there was no way to climb out. If the fall didn't kill, starvation did. There were other means of human sacrifice represented, none of it humane.

The Maya were also sports minded, as evidenced by a huge stone ring mounted high on a wall for a team sport – perhaps a precursor to basketball. We were also told that at the spring and autumn equinox, during the rising and setting of the sun, one could observe along the pyramid's edge the undulating shadow of a serpent.

There was so much more of interest to see but on such group tours, it is wise not to be left behind. Our Mexican adventure too short, we headed back to the bus and our ship.

When in Spain

In 1966, we saw an advertisement extolling Spain's virtues as a travel destination. By now, we had survived four Florida vacations and one to Mexico and were confident that Spain would be easy. Ahhh, but it stands to reason that anyone arriving in Acapulco at midnight without a peso (only U.S. Traveler's cheques) and with no reservations, would be likely candidates to come unravelled in Spain. The most immediate setback was that, although it was shortly after 2:00 a.m. by our biological clocks, it was 8:00 a.m. at the airport, and the day was just beginning in Madrid.

Our arrival was not exactly of the "Wheee, we're in Spain!" genre, due largely to the fact that Renaud was headachy, feverish and his chest hurt. My sympathy for him was tinged with a touch of serves-you-right, because I knew his indisposition was a direct result of a long St. Anicet Winter Carnival weekend directly before departure, during the course of which he coached the old-timer's hockey team at the school's outdoor rink in a raging blizzard, comforted by a pint of gin to keep his radiator from freezing.

Further complicating our arrival in Sunny Spain was our belief that it really would be sunny and since we had recently cottoned onto the "travel light" system, (a direct result of a suitcase confrontation), we had nothing better than thin raincoats to protect us from the cold and penetrating February drizzle in progress when we touched down at Madrid International.

Pepe, a lithe, cheerful Spanish taxi driver, hovered around us at the terminal until he was sure we were as lost as we looked, then adopted us, attaching himself like a benevolent barnacle. Pepe found a room for us at a large midtown hotel, outlined an ambitious sightseeing agenda, and took over the matter of our care and cultural enlightenment. He was very patient, a wonderful guide. Our Spain experience was made memorable by his expertise and kindness.

Pepe had a fortunate flair for language, boundless energy and enormous national pride. A dapper little guy (a Spanish-style ringer for Sammy Davis, Jr.), Pepe had a pleasant, chatty way and was determined that we should love and appreciate his country as much as he did.

Every day, Pepe came to the hotel for us and drove us somewhere elegant or historical. He was justifiably stunned whenever Renaud, still in misery, chose to remain huddled in the back seat of his cab while I skimmed quickly through castles and other tourist attractions, in order to cover as much territory as possible because I was aware, if Pepe wasn't, that our days in Spain were probably numbered less than our airline tickets promised.

We travelled the countryside in the rain with Pepe gallantly giving us his proud travelogue. We toured Queen Isabella's castle and Pepe pointed out bridges, castles on mountain peaks and storks nesting on rooftop chimneys.

Lifting Renaud's dark mood was like lifting the iron curtain, so Pepe apologized for the rain, and said that his friend Antonio had a villa for rent on the Mediterranean. He would drive us there, where it would surely be sunny.

We were game. The next morning, Pepe arrived at our hotel with his wife, Isabel, whom we had agreed should come along. Loading our two small suitcases into the trunk of Pepe's car, we headed south, toward Torremolinos.

Driving up hills, down hills, and between hills, we crouched along ravines, sped recklessly around pointy little mountains and through small-town clusters of adobe-type dwellings reposing in mid-day siesta.

Renaud dozed, occasionally glancing up wanly whenever I nudged him with my elbow to get his attention. Pepe was a confident driver and he whisked us smoothly past shepherds tending their flocks and windmills perched picturesquely on hillsides throughout Don Quixote's Le Mancha countryside.

We sped past miles of Spain's lush countryside, replete with rolling, dark brown velvet fields set with endless neat rows of spiky, sleeping grape vines, making the voluptuously rounded hills look remarkably like matronly bosoms studded with dark sequins. The sun came out for about 10 minutes during the drive south, but by the time we reached Malaga and Torremolinos, we were in a relentless downpour.

After meeting Pepe's Antonio and settling into our villa, right on the boardwalk along the Mediterranean, Renaud and I smiled and agreed that of course there would be sunshine tomorrow. He felt well again, and looked forward to exploring the surroundings. Still, I had qualms about whether or not that would make a difference. After all, it was sunny in Acapulco, too, and look what happened.

In our charming, small, yellow-trimmed, white stuccoed concrete villa overlooking the sea, evenings were spent huddled close to each other and to the portable gas heater crouched in the middle of the living room-kitchen floor.

We concluded that since the villa had probably been closed for months, it would take a while to warm up. It never did. Not that night nor the other days and nights that followed.

True, Antonio's villa off-season at $4.00 a day was incredibly inexpensive but it was made of concrete block, and soon after we took up residence, we discovered that its chief characteristic was that it lent credence to the old saying, "cold as a tomb."

Pushing the twin beds together at night, we retired early, wearing the entire contents of our two small suitcases. We never stopped shivering. The bed sheets were cold and damp; our feet were freezing, even with socks and slippers on. The concrete walls were sweaty, and so icy that when bare skin accidentally brushed against them, we shrieked.

Walking to the bathroom in the middle of the night wasn't any worse than visiting the outhouse in dead of winter as our pioneer Canadian forefathers did. Each day, when the morning sky lightened to a heavy gray, we reluctantly crawled out of our body-heat warmed hive to do nothing.

Still it rained. We looked hopefully for Local Colour, but it was too shrouded in rain to find. On our strolls along the boardwalk, we peered into the windows of small stores patiently awaiting rain-soaked customers. Brightly painted fishing boats sat hauled up on the sandy expanse of beach, and hungry cats lounged in sheltered alleys, watching hopefully as fishermen, in preparation for better weather, silently straightened, mended and folded nets in the lea of small buildings. It was, indeed, picturesque, but without sunshine.

From the moment of our arrival in Spain, mealtime was a problem. It wasn't easy to get the hang of when Spaniards ate. It wasn't like North America, where we take it for granted that most restaurants are open all day long, and mealtime is whenever you want it to be. We soon discovered that whenever our Canadian stomachs yelped "Hungry!" Spain's restaurants were closed tight as a fist.

Restaurants were open in the evening for dinner. They were, as anticipated, what might be expected of Spain: checkered tablecloths and pitchers of sangria; white damask, crystal. Of course, there were never translated menus. Our little pocket English/Spanish dictionary didn't work all that well, so ordering was difficult, except when Pepe was with us.

On tours with Pepe, who had a penchant for smart restaurants, we managed to eat, but unfortunately, no matter how quaint the decor, or how great the bread and wine, the meat was always too young for our tastes and the vegetables were overcooked.

My cousin and her husband spend time in Spain every winter and are particularly fond of that country's cuisine but Renaud and I just didn't get it. Spain's restaurants, at least the ones near us, were never open for breakfast, and seldom for lunch. Because the furnishings in our little villa kitchen consisted of only two wooden chairs (there was no table) we managed our breakfasts, eaten out of hand, of instant coffee with powdered coffee creamer brought from home, and rusk and jam from a nearby corner store.

Because of our sparse breakfasts and non-existent lunches, we made sure to find restaurants for dinner. It took alertness to understand the workings of Spain's mealtimes.

Even Pepe's explanations about afternoon siesta because of the hot sun (Sun? What sun?) were not enough to keep us from always being hungry at the wrong time, and wanting to be in bed by Spain's dinner time.

We soon became used to two restaurants within lunging-through-the-rain distance of our concrete villa. One restaurant's specialty was a very bony but delicious fish that came to a small stand next to our table in a rectangular container that housed a big salt block. The waiter carefully chipped away at this salt block with a hammer, until the fish could be lifted out and served.

This restaurant sat on a corner, facing the high street. It filled early with dinner-hour customers, who were joyously entertained by a clutch of troubadours squeezing between tables and chairs and singing cheerfully and loudly, right in the ears of the diners, undoubtedly in celebration of what Pepe had proclaimed as "...the end of the longest drought in Spain's history," that heralded our arrival.

A larger restaurant, midway down the boardwalk, had more space between the tables, no troubadours, a better menu, and a mammoth fireplace.

In this restaurant, a wall of windows overlooked the boardwalk and the Mediterranean, though all we could see as we sat huddled next to the orange glow of the blazing

hearth was dense gray and black clouds beyond the colourful, beached fishing boats, and rain sluicing thickly down
the great expanse of glass. We spent as much time as con-
science allowed in this restaurant, pressed as close to the
crackling fire as possible.

Our raincoats didn't get a chance to dry, acting instead
as wicks, so that when we retrieved them after our leisurely
dinners, they hurriedly soaked into the partially dried and
warmed-by-the-fireside clothes we were wearing. Defeated
and damp, we trailed from the cozy restaurant, returning to
the cold villa for another night of shivering. Our faces were
long indeed and, if I didn't always hear Renaud hum-hum-
ming grimly, it was only because the thrum of rain drowned
him out.

II
GETTING THERE

Retreat to Florida

In Spain, we didn't understand why, in spite of the rain, and being off-season, there were still a lot of tourists. They filled the restaurants. They trod briskly along the boardwalk en route to mysterious destinations, carried umbrellas and wore thick, warm coats under vinyl capes and raincoats. They wore rubber boots. They were prepared. Why weren't *we* prepared? Why didn't *we* know?

On the fourth morning of cold rusk toast and powdered coffee with powdered milk, Renaud put his arm around my shoulders as we huddled together over the gas heater in the icy kitchen-living room and said "Enough is enough! I'm going to Florida, where it's warm!"

I wasn't about to argue. Escaping winter was one thing, but trading it for the rainy season was not our intention. Florida! But we couldn't get there from Torremolinos, so first, back to Madrid. I washed the cups, tucked them into their little cupboard and we put on our damp raincoats and left the villa.

Along the boardwalk, we walked briskly past packs of cats sitting in sheltered doorways looking intently, with narrowed, longing eyes at the beached fishing boats. We made our way up to the high street, flagged a cruising taxi and indicated to the Spanish taxi driver, by pointing to the sky and flapping our arms, that we wanted to go to the airport in Malaga.

After buying two tickets on the afternoon flight to Madrid, we hailed another cab and returned to Torremolinos. Drawing a clock face on the back of the ticket folder, we showed our driver what time we wanted to be picked up and driven back to the airport for our flight.

Sprinting down to the boardwalk through the rain and into our villa with buoyant spirits, we said good-bye to Antonio and his family, and packed our bags.

Back at the airport, we entered the funny little plane through a tail door. A strip of canvas separated the passengers from the flight deck, and there were, so help me, dangling overhead straps under the baggage rack. It looked like a Disney movie flying bus.

Minutes after landing in Madrid, we phoned Pepe, who picked us up and drove us to the C.P. Air Office to change our 30-day tickets so we could leave, hopefully, right away. We explained to the clerk, with Pepe's help, that we didn't want to continue our holiday (implying that not only the rain was all their fault, but St. Anicet Winter Carnival as well).

We also learned that we could not fly directly to Florida, because we were Canadians. We had to fly to Canada first. So, we bought tickets to take us to Montreal.

Renaud wanted to leave Spain immediately, but finally agreed to wait for the plane. This meant 2 more days in Madrid.

Pepe returned us to our former Madrid hotel and suggested that if we didn't have plans, he would be happy to drive us north to Segovia the next morning for some sightseeing. We agreed.

 After supper, we went to our room, hung our raincoats near the radiator to dry, and went to bed. We slept well that night. We were warm.

Next morning, on the way to Segovia with Pepe, rain turned to snow. In Segovia, it turned to rain again. For lunch, Pepe took us to an ancient establishment next to the still functioning 2000-year-old Roman Aqueduct. Dominating the surroundings the famous aqueduct was clearly a major example of no mortar, granite block architecture. Pepe pulled over and stopped the car as we approached. The imposing view of double rows of arches marching off into the distance was stunning. Pepe watched us, saw our amazement, smiled, and gave us a brief history of the aqueduct. Then we proceeded to the nearby restaurant he had chosen for our lunch.

The restaurant was in a very, very old building, but it was cozy and warm, with open-hearth, spit roasting in the informal downstairs dining area. The windows were small, the walls very old wood. Pepe arranged for us to be served in the more formal dining area upstairs. Ascending the narrow and steep old staircase, single file, our knees banged into the steps ahead.

Sitting at a table in front of the upstairs dining room fireplace, we talked to Pepe about Canada, answering his questions about winter blizzards and ice-skating until our meal came. The waiter placed a young joint of goat leg in front of Renaud, where it extended off both sides of his plate. My vegetable platter arrived drenched in oil. The bread was wonderful, and the sangria superb.

In Madrid, later in the afternoon, Pepe left us at our hotel and promised to drive us to the airport the next day. With a couple of daylight hours to fill, we strolled along the busy rain-streaked sidewalks of Madrid. It looked like a picture postcard. Thanks to Pepe, we experienced Spain in spite of the weather. Castles, windmills, storks, Roman aqueduct, the Mediterranean, troubadours and sangria. But, still we looked ahead to the glowing warm promise of Florida dangling before us like a carrot. Soon ...

Suddenly, a neat, housewifey-looking woman wearing a navy blue, belted raincoat and carrying a black leather purse stepped out of the shelter of a doorway and approached us. Speaking quickly, in Spanish, she addressed Renaud who shrugged and said he didn't understand. She held a card out to him. We looked at it, but that too was in Spanish. Thinking she might be selling lottery tickets, or collecting for something, we waved her off, and continued our walk.

Later, on the way back to our hotel, another woman, of similar neatness, approached and tried to strike up a conversation with Renaud. He smiled encouragingly. That was all she needed, because she then grasped his arm and pulled. Since I had hold of his other arm, a sort of tug-of-war ensued. She pulled and babbled on in Spanish, I pulled and said "Hey–hey–HEY..."

Renaud looked surprised, but not alarmed. Perhaps it wouldn't be stretching things to say he looked a trifle flattered at this contest, and, in fact, didn't seem to be putting up much of a fight for himself. Eventually he turned away, pulling his arm free, and the woman left.

Pepe explained the next morning on the way to the airport that the woman of the streets probably assumed I was another member of her trade and she was going to take the nice looking man away from me. Just goes to show that we all look alike in navy blue raincoats.

Back in our hotel room, we hung our wet clothing on chair backs to dry overnight. After a comforting shower, then dinner in the hotel dining room, we returned to our room and crawled thankfully into our warm bed. Rain sluiced softly against the windows. "I'll bet," I said, snuggling down into all the lovely warmth that central heat and a good husband provide, "I'll just bet that because we're leaving here tomorrow, you'll see, the sun will shine and it will be a beautiful day." It didn't, and it wasn't.

It was still raining after breakfast as we put on our almost dry raincoats and went down to the lobby to meet Pepe and drive to the airport.

Back home, in Canada's cold and snow, we had a quick family get-together, did a laundry, got a restless night's sleep, loaded the car and headed south.

I said, "Shouldn't we phone Vito first and see if he has a room?"

Renaud said, "Aw, don't worry, he'll find something for us." And he did.

B. Cool

So, how did our travels really start? How did we break the pattern of "All work and no play" to become happy, if inept, holidayers? Certainly, it began a few years before Mexico and Spain.

On a routine Sunday afternoon in January 1961, after 8 years without a break, an impulsive decision started the ball rolling. The children were all under 7, the business was still struggling and we'd had no time off alone, together, since our first anniversary red-teardrop-trailer adventure of 1953.

Setting our after-dinner mugs of coffee on the gravity-flow oil furnace straddling the archway between living room and kitchen, we pulled our chairs closer to the warmth. Billy and Joey played car racing on loops of track-roadways running from kitchen to living room, hurling themselves at Happy, our dog, whenever he pounced on the cars.

The baby, Linda, was in her playpen, laughing at the action. Snow plopped in heavy, moist clumps against the windows, more snow hung in white garlands, bracketing a chorus line of thick icicles, and darkening the house so that the lights had to be left on all day.

Another week of the usual winter routine of sending the grader out to clear roads and setting the mechanics to repairing farm tractors and equipment as well as construction equipment in readiness for spring.

Renaud drank his coffee slowly, and in silence. Then, setting his empty cup gently but deliberately on top of the furnace, he looked at me and, over the din of the children's

49

raucous play, leaned toward my ear and said, with a desperate edge to his voice, "Let's go to Florida."

I said, "You bet!" and "When?"

Renaud paused, looked thoughtful, and then said "Wednesday!"

"Which Wednesday?" I asked.

"This Wednesday," he said.

"This Wednesday?"

"Yes."

"That's only three days away," I said.

"I know," he said.

Back in our red-tear-drop trailer days, it was easy. We were younger and childless. There were few bills and fewer responsibilities. No one back then depended on us, and the only things we had to make arrangements for were two goldfish and a geranium. And they weren't complaining.

But 8 years of struggle took their toll. We were parents now. Responsible, serious, tired. And another hard summer lay ahead beyond three more months of snow, ice and frozen water pipes. Could we really drop everything for a midwinter southern holiday? I said, "I'll be ready."

We made decisions, phone calls, and more decisions. Happy, our dog, would go to the Dog and Cat Motel, a boarding kennel 5 miles down the road, and Putt-Putt, our cat, would go on mouser duty at the office.

That night, I lay sleepless in bed, mentally organizing the household for our absence. What lucky friends/relatives would get custody of the children, Pinkey the hamster, the ant farm and the rubber tree? What would I pack, and in what, for the children? And the pets. And if you don't believe you have to pack for a hamster, let me tell you about seeds, hamster pellets, treats, cedar shavings, paper towels, cage-liners, and oil for his squeaking treadmill. Pinkey would not board out without his little necessities.

As soon as Renaud left for work the next morning, the boys got into their car racing again. I carried dishes to the bathroom sink (kitchen pipes frozen), stepping high over the car tracks snaking across the floor.

I washed the dishes, carried them back to the kitchen, dried them, and stowed them in the cupboards. Then I pulled my old tweed suitcase full of the boys' summer shorts and shirts from the attic and emptied it into a cardboard box. As I picked lint out of the corners of the suitcase, the televised weather report concluded with the announcer saying, "Well, travellers, do we have a treat for you! Stay tuned..." Hummm, did he say travellers? A program of travel hints? Well, if ever someone needed travel hints....

As the commercials ran their course, I settled a sibling outbreak over a collision, slipped a clean jersey over Linda's head and took her out of her high chair and into the bedroom for her nap. Then I scrambled through the junk drawer for a pad and pen.

Commercial over, the program host came on screen to say that his featured guest, Mrs. B. Cool, (of course not her real name) was here to give expert advice on travel. I could hardly wait. How timely! A real expert to offer sage counsel and help me decide what to wear, what to bring, what to leave behind and how to pack efficiently.

The telephone interrupted. I answered. It was Renaud.

"Margie," he said.

"Yes?" I answered.

"Guess what."

"What?"

"About Florida..."

"What about Florida?"

"Uh, Ma and Pa have never been to Florida."

"Oh," I said. "And...?"

"They're coming with us," he said. Thus, in the eternal way Caza men have of doing things, began another tradition.

I replaced the telephone thoughtfully. Our first vacation in eight years. Not exactly what I had planned, but not a bad thing considering they were such amiable in-laws. I poured another cup of coffee, set it next to the pad and pen on the table, and sat down to see if this television program would improve my capacity to travel smartly.

After a final commercial, the host explained that Mrs. Cool was a career woman who travelled extensively. She was, he said, the ultimate expert on the subject of travel, and was now preparing herself for a 5-day business trip to Europe. What's more, Mrs. Cool would make her entrance to the studio in her entire travel wardrobe, carrying everything she needed, unaided.

After this build-up, I half expected a comic figure to emerge, swamped with half a dozen suitcases, one of which would fall to the floor and have to be kicked ahead as Mrs. Cool advanced. If this wasn't to be a serious program on travel advice, that was OK by me. I was ready to be entertained. I waited for B. Cool to make her bumbling entrance.

The music swelled, the camera picked up the curtains stage left, and Mrs. Cool swept into the studio. Pausing dramatically, she twirled around, glided elegantly forward and shook hands with the host. This was no cartoon character. Mrs. Cool looked absolutely stunning.

Mrs. Cool's concept of travelling light was equally stunning. There was no suitcase. Her purse was a soft, rich looking, plump leather briefcase. What she carried, and what she wore into the studio was evidently it – her complete travel wardrobe for 5 days.

She sat down, crossed her long, slim legs neatly, and looked about with a charming smile. I knew a childish moment of wanting to kick her in the shins.

Mrs. Cool was tall, with a long, thin, small-boned, Miss America figure. She had that slick, professional look common to high-class models that suck in their cheeks and pout their moistened lips.

Obviously, Mrs. B. Cool was an expert for the experts, not for the humble masses. It was clear that she knew nothing about arranging for three children and their pets, or about missing the kids and driving in a car in need of a good tune-up. I was equally sure she had never experienced torn underwear, pinned-up hems, ratty winter nightgowns with too-short long sleeves, spilled cereal, dirty diapers, frozen plumbing, or impossible budgets.

I looked at my uneven fingernails, rough cuticles, and chapped knuckles. I was glad Renaud wasn't around to compare me to this svelte vision of organization and pampered salon good looks.

Mrs. Cool wore a black maxi-dress, and a high-crowned, wide-brimmed black hat. She did not wear a coat, but I had a strong feeling that there might be a mink lurking backstage. She had that look about her.

The demonstration began. Chatting animatedly, Mrs. Cool withdrew a handful of smart costume jewellery from her briefcase, and then unfurled a tumble of silk scarves, some muted, some vibrantly coloured. Her dress seemed to be built (yes, built) with discretely placed snaps, tabs and hooks to accommodate alterations with diamond and gold clips for neckline, shoulder and arm draping to alter her ensemble for different effects.

As a stunning finale – you won't believe this – Mrs. Cool stood up and ripped the flared bottom six inches off her dress to the accompaniment of shrieks and gasps from the studio audience, followed by applause as, lo and behold, within seconds the dress was transformed, thanks to Velcro tape, to a short, smart afternoon dress.

The audience was duly impressed. I was, too. But morning talk show hosts should be told that it's not fair to present a beautiful, organized, self-assured, well-endowed (physically and undoubtedly financially) person to advise housewife television viewers, most of whom don't have the same basic equipment.

I have the same outraged feeling when I see leggy movie-star types advertising panty hose, brazenly assuring their audience that they, too, can look just as great – if they buy the same brand. It doesn't work. I tried.

I poured another cup of coffee and watched an inspiring oven-cleaning commercial that was more my speed.

When the host returned he smiled fatuously. "Oh, this is wonderful!" he gushed. "Mrs. Cool," he went on coyly, "You're so beautifully organized. But what, if you don't mind my asking, if you get a run in your nylons? And what about uh, fresh underwear, and uh, nightwear? And what else do you carry in that, umm, briefcase?"

Pleased to no end with these questions, Mrs. Cool opened the briefcase: a small make-up case, a small umbrella, a small purse, evening sandals and a business portfolio.

She then retrieved her broad-brimmed, high-crowned hat from the coffee table, where she had tossed it a few minutes earlier, flipped it over, lifted a flap inside the crown, and out tumbled the flimsies. Nylon stockings, undies, wispy nylon nightie, sheer blouse. Everything, she explained, colour-coordinated, feather-light and drip-dry. No problem.

Well, maybe she didn't have any problems, but Mrs. Cool's version of travel was enough for me. I snapped up pencil and pad, tossed them back into the junk drawer (I'll bet Mrs. Cool doesn't even *have* a junk drawer), turned off the television, and grimly set about packing in my own way, and, although I harboured some resentment toward Mrs. B. Cool and her travel smarts, I couldn't help but giggle at the thought of Renaud's reaction to me preparing for our vacation by stuffing my pink flowered flannelette granny gown into the crown of my $4.98 beige straw hat.

Just Bring One Suitcase

Mrs. B. Cool's advice wasn't much help, but at least she started me thinking about preparations for our trip south. Our packing dilemma never lessened over the years because I was a try-to-bring-everything-we-might-need person and Renaud was convinced that he could leave home to spend a month anywhere with a toothbrush in one pocket and a spare pair of socks in the other. Not that he was going to stay anywhere for a whole month anyway – unless it was Florida.

The key here is to realize that Renaud, like a cleaning lady who doesn't do windows, was a traveller who wanted nothing to do with luggage. He dealt with it, of course, but like most of us he didn't want to pack it, stow it in the car, carry it, check it at airports, or wait for it anywhere.

However, somebody had to do it because all that loose talk on his part about only needing a toothbrush and a spare pair of socks fell somewhat short of reality when he was looking for a clean shirt.

There was more to preparing to go on holiday than figuring out what to pack. There was the matter of organizing everything that had to be left behind. This called for lists. Lists reminded me to arrange the dog's stay at the kennel, and the cat's stay at the office. Lists kept me from packing three tubes of toothpaste and forgetting the tooth brushes. They reminded me to include a pack of playing cards, in case we got stuck in transit.

Lists were also practical as they allowed me to check off things as they went into the suitcase – although the first time I did that I crossed the items out so heavily that I couldn't see what I had crossed off, and kept duplicating by scribbling already packed things at the bottom of the list.

I've always been the sort of absent-minded person who did such things as put the roast on the ironing board and the neatly rolled bundle of dampened laundry into the oven; the kind of person who would lower herself into a tub of hot, soapy water with her shoes on, and the sort of person strangers picked lint off. The sort of person the inventor of the pen with a headlight probably had in mind. At night I would lie awake thinking of things that still had to be done before leaving, knowing that they were sure to sweep past recall if I got up to look for pen and paper. I've always depended upon lists to keep us on track.

Lists were also important because whatever's been forgotten, whether my address book, beach robe, summer purse, or Renaud's electric razor, favorite golf shirt or bathing suit (probably left hanging on the doorknob of the spare room at home since August) was my responsibility.

Renaud always claimed that luggage, although necessary, was a nuisance. Still, a necessary nuisance. Something to be concerned about.

For instance, we worried about our luggage that time when we had three flight connections. We worried about our luggage when we missed connections and had to stay overnight in Atlanta and sleep in our underwear while our bags spent the night in limbo. And we certainly worried about more than our luggage the time our plane blew an engine shortly after takeoff and caught fire.

And of course there was the matter of time wasted waiting for luggage, and the difficulty of keeping it together and carrying it around.

Finally, after one particularly stormy luggage-complicated vacation, Renaud put his foot down. "One suitcase," he said, patiently but firmly.

It was 1965. We were in the kitchen at the time, examining our tickets and Mexican itinerary. I put the tickets in our passport folder and looked at him absently. "One suitcase?" I asked. "What do you mean, one suitcase?"

"Just bring one suitcase," he repeated.

"Each?" I asked.

"No," he said, "One suitcase altogether – for both of us."

I said "But..." He said, "If you think I'm going to haul half a dozen bags all over Mexico..."

I said, "I'm a reasonable person. I don't want half a dozen bags either. But one?"

As chief packer and bag-organizer, I know there are things we will need if we're going to stay in Mexico for a month. Even if Renaud does drag out his famous logic that "We can always buy what we need when we get there."

The point is, those who issue ultimatums must learn to face consequences, because instead of wasting time arguing about this new one-suitcase edict I went suitcase shopping.

Cost, an important consideration, I ignored the exclusive Traveller's Boutique, with its quality luggage, and headed for the bargain-luggage section, in search of the biggest, cheapest suitcase I could find, short of a trunk.

There, ta-da, I found Big Red -- red canvas and the approximate size of a zip-top St. Bernard. It was big, even by my standards. Sitting there in the midst of the luggage department, surrounded by all manner of hanging bags, wheeling bags, trunks and matched sets endowed this red canvas monster with a certain in-store, travel-bound legitimacy – though it still stood out like a merry-go-round in a cathedral.

I bought it, of course. Forcing it into the car, I was surprised to discover that it took up the entire back seat. Still, it wasn't until it slumped over apologetically in the middle of our small living room that I felt a real twinge of apprehension.

Once the actual packing was underway, it was rather amazing to see just how much Big Red could hold. It held a lot. However, as I loaded it I realized that this huge, soft-sided red bag had no frame or support. It just sort of became bloated. Like hamster cheeks – big hamster cheeks.

The more I packed, the more I thought, "Renaud's not going to like this," so I made darn sure he didn't set eyes on it until it was time to leave for the airport. Of course, by then it was too late to do anything about it. It was almost too late to fight about it – but not quite.

And it didn't take long for me to regret my cleverness, because that red canvas monstrosity was embarrassingly conspicuous. It presented us with a dead weight that refused to stand neatly or be carried jauntily. It did all but wheeze asthmatically as Renaud, silent, but glowering darkly, towed it across airport lobbies (no wheels), yanked it into taxis, heaved it up on luggage platforms and later dragged it off the carrousels with looks that threatened bagicide and worse if I even tried to explain.

We had to wait just as long at customs and other places as we would have with two smaller, easy to manage bags. Besides that, people, total strangers, laughed.

The year after the St. Bernard suitcase fiasco, while preparing for Spain, Renaud was ominously quiet about vacation plans until two days before our flight. Then he put his hands gently but firmly on my shoulders, looked me straight in the eyes and said, in a patient voice, "About the luggage. Get rid of that big red thing. I don't want us to bring more than we can carry easily and inconspicuously." I was ready.

In fact, as soon as we had returned from Mexico, I gave the red canvas beast away and bought two lightweight, 20-inch bags. That's what we have travelled with ever since. It's been enough. Well, of course, we nearly froze in Spain and in England – sweaters take too much room.

In the beginning, I was no smarter about choosing the things that go into suitcases than I was about buying them. But I learned. I learned that buying the large, economy size of necessities may be thrifty at home, but it's not smart for travelling. For years, when travelling by car, with a nice, roomy trunk, I practiced the false economy of packing half-pound tubes of toothpaste and super-economy size deodorant.

I stopped such economies and switched to small, one-trip size, lightweight plastic containers after the time

I packed a huge glass bottle of Palmolive shampoo, bought on sale. It broke the first day on the road south, saturating the entire contents of one suitcase (yes, mine) with slimy green perfumed liquid. Picking out chunks and slivers of glass, and rinsing out everything in the motel bath tub, to the accompaniment of foam, bubbles, prevailing scent and patient looks and head-shakes from Renaud (when I should have been relaxing with him with half of the daily newspaper and a gin and tonic before supper) was a stern lesson.

Sometimes, I looked toward the advice of travel professionals like Ms. Cool, and Fromm's "Europe on $10.00 a day" (This was in the '60s) for packing tips, but I learned that the experts don't always have both feet on the ground.

Especially the expert who recommended methods of packing dressy shoes, extra suits, evening wear, ties, etc., then suggested that travellers use raincoats to lounge about in, or to toddle down the hall to the bathroom in. (Yes, in those early travel days there wasn't always an en-suite bathroom).

True, a multipurpose raincoat might well save packing space, but an enveloping housecoat or bathrobe, even if it is thin and squashed, has earned priority. It's worth its suitcase space in the gold of solid comfort when coming in after a busy, cool or rainy day. And it's nothing short of luxury to get a shower and relax with a cosiness no raincoat could allow. Especially if that raincoat is wet. And why wouldn't it be wet? It is, after all, a raincoat.

Renaud didn't want us to take a lot with us on short holidays. "Just the suit I have on is all I'm going to need," he would insist. When we were preparing for a four-day Las Vegas jaunt in 1982, to a heavy-equipment convention, all he wanted to take was one carry-on bag for both of us. That was all right in concept, but the reality went something like this:

"Oh, don't forget my razor."

I said "Of course not."

"What if it gets cold? Perhaps I should bring a sweater." I agreed. After all, we're older now, I remembered Spain in February, and I'd heard that desert nights are chilly.

"Hummm, and a long-sleeved shirt too. Just in case. Maybe an extra pair of socks," he added.

It made sense. I added the shirt and socks.

"I think," said Renaud. "I should take my slippers along, they're so comfortable. Do you have room?"

I said, "Yes," and started a second carry-on bag.

"Don't forget my razor."

"I've already packed it."

"Uuuhh, handkerchiefs?"

"They're packed."

"I was just wondering about those red shorts I bought last year in Palm Beach. You know, with the yellow stripe. Do you know where they are?"

"Right here."

Then I said, "I think I'll take along my camera, in case we go back to Hoover Dam."

And he said, "Well, don't pack too much now. Remember, we don't want a lot of luggage." How could I forget?

∞∞∞∞

As we continued to travel lighter and lighter, with only carry-ons for short trips, the freedom of no luggage to check or wait for was wonderful. Even when, one January day we took off from Montreal's Dorval Airport in a blizzard, made an unscheduled landing in New York's LaGuardia, then on to Raleigh, North Carolina, where the fog was so dense we approached bumpily to make an instrument landing.

The pilot said, "Well, we're going to land. I don't know where, because if we can't see anything 200 feet from the ground, we'll have to go back up and try to get in at Charlotte."

We did get in at Raleigh, landing too firmly for comfort. "Sorry about that, folks, but I just worked to get us down in one piece and didn't try for anything fancy," said the pilot with false heartiness.

It was 11 p.m., and our Atlanta connection had waited.

"Gate B-6," the harried officer in the lounge told us, checking passengers off the list of flights that had been held back, and we scurried along without a care in the world – with just our carry-ons.

The announcement that greeted us on board was "Next stop, Miami!" We didn't get into Ft. Lauderdale until two in the morning.

"Didn't I tell you that no-checked-luggage was the sensible way?" said Renaud. I had to admit he was right.

Auto-Train

It was 1974. We were driving south on the Washington Beltway after a beans and franks lunch at Howard Johnson's on our second day out. Our son Joey, 16, and daughter Linda, 14, were in the back seat. The sun shone warmly through the car windows.

I was in the midst of a satisfying stretch and yawn when suddenly a sign stood out bold and clear. "Auto-Train, Exit 1 mile," and I said, "Humm, we should try that some time, Renaud."

"Want to?" he asked.

I said "Sure," and we pulled over onto the exit ramp.

The kids were delighted, of course. And so was I, because I love train travel. Besides, anyone who says "...getting there is half the fun" has never travelled from Canada to Florida by car with a husband who stuck to the speed limit, insisted on getting up at 6 a.m. to put in a couple of hours driving before breakfast, and stopped at gas stations only when gas was really needed.

Add to that my position as navigator and tendency to doze off and get us lost, and you have a splendid motive to look for alternatives.

The timing was perfect. The car yard of the Auto-Train compound was almost empty, the train, snorting in readiness for departure, directly in front of us.

A man in overalls directed cars toward a carrier ramp. We stopped and asked if we could book on. He said, "You're in luck. There's been a bad snow storm in Ohio, and lots of cancellations."

Renaud asked, "What do we do?"

"Get what you need for overnight from your car," he said. "Then leave your keys with me. Pay in the office, over there." He added, "We're leaving in half an hour."

We didn't ask how much it would cost, but had we been less impulsive we might have taken into consideration that we were with our own children instead of with another, expense-sharing couple, and we would have to pay for the whole thing.

Giddy with the thought of this new adventure, we laughed and joked while fishing toothbrushes and sweaters from the trunk of the car. Seconds later, we were in the ticketing office, and by the time we learned the cost for 4 adults and a car it was too late to back down. Through the big picture window in the office, we watched our car being driven smartly aboard. Renaud sighed and pulled out our traveller's cheques.

I tried to comfort him as we climbed on board and were ushered to the upper level of our assigned car, number 8. "Uh, Renaud, that includes supper tonight and breakfast tomorrow," I said.

"Yeah, yeah..." he responded glumly.

"And we'll save on gas, and oil, and wear and tear on the tires, too," I reminded him as we settled into our upper-level, day-nighter seats with Joey and Linda in the seats across the aisle.

"And you can take it easy," I said. "You won't be driving."

"Uh-huh," he grunted.

"And don't forget," I reminded him brightly. "We won't have the expense of a motel tonight."

Renaud muttered something about "Ten motels would have been cheaper than this."

Joey said, "We'll be right near Disney World when we wake up in the morning."

"And you can sleep," I said.

"Well, it's not too bad, I suppose," said Renaud.

We were on our way.

The hostess came around to see if we were comfortable and to answer questions. She said that below us was a full-car-size lounge and bar for card-playing, smoking, partying and general stay-up-all-night, merry-making.

She said there were fewer than half the usual 400 passengers on board because of a winter blizzard that shut down Ohio, that we were cutting out 900 road miles by using Auto-Train, that we would be travelling 17 hours, that the Auto-Train had 40 passenger cars and covered car-carriers, that our speed would average 60 mph, and we would arrive at Sanford, Florida, 29 miles from Disney World, by 9:00 the next morning.

She added that we must choose early or late sitting for supper, that there would be a movie in the dining room after supper, and that the 'Starlight Room Night Club' was four cars back. She gave us each a blanket and pillow and went on to the next passenger.

I looked at Renaud with some concern. He was very quiet, gazing off into space, massaging his stomach. "Are you all right?" I asked, He moaned. I put a pillow behind his head, pulled up his footrest, and tucked a blanket around him. He promptly shut his eyes. I knew he wasn't asleep though because, every once in a while, he patted his stomach and moan.

Tired of watching scenery zip by, Linda and Joey launched on an exploration of the train, I settled into reading Auto-Train brochures.

Uniformed hosts and hostesses glided along the carpeted aisles, being solicitous and dispensing information, advice, good will, and playing cards. They were doing their best, but I doubted very much if they had the means to un-grump a husband who had eaten beans for lunch and had just laid out an unexpectedly large portion of cash at the beginning of our vacation.

I hoped Renaud's mood would lighten when we went to supper, but although the dining car atmosphere was calm and unhurried and the table bore a soothingly elegant linen tablecloth, napkins, candles, and real flowers, and the meal was well-presented roast chicken, followed by fruit and cheese tray and coffee, Renaud still looked quietly miserable.

After supper Joey, Linda and I said we wanted to check out the Starlight Lounge. Renaud was reluctant, but a good sport, so the four of us jostled our way along the corridors from car to car until we found the upper level nightclub on wheels.

We leaned back in the deep upholstery, legs stretched out, and ordered coffee for us, and 7-up for the kids. Ah, it was really nice. Here we were, covering the miles while rocking gently to the accompaniment of a guitar-playing singer whose unflagging cheer led him, in spite of what appeared to be a severe head cold, through Lennon, Dylan, Gershwin, Porter, and many others. After 'Feelings,' 'Sunshine,' 'Comin' 'round the Mountain,' 'Homeward Bound,' 'You Light up my Life,' and Croche's wistful 'Time in a Bottle,' a hostess brought around submarine sandwiches and more coffee and Renaud said, "You stay here if you want, but I'm going back to our seats."

He did, and an hour or so later the kids and I followed to snuggle down into pillows and blankets in our tweed-covered, colour-coordinated recliners. Renaud was still awake. I cuddled into my blanket to enjoy the ride. We swayed easily to the clickity-click-clickity-click of the wheels, and I dozed occasionally, listening to the whoooo-whooooo of the train whistle, and musical ding-ding-ding-ding monotone of level crossing signals, recalling railroad adventure stories of my youth. Ah, the romance of the rails....

We woke up around 7 a.m. in Florida with time to wash, smooth our wrinkled, slept-in clothes and do a few stretches in the aisle before having a leisurely continental breakfast while sweeping past orange groves in Florida's misty early morning sunshine. By 9 a.m., we were at the Sanford terminal, where the cars were unloaded. Renaud by now was feeling better so it was on to Disney World.

Pilot to Navigator

What I liked most about the Auto-Train was that I wasn't navigator. I never liked being navigator. Especially for someone who's convinced that road maps are not only unnecessary, but a disadvantage. No wonder we weren't able to travel two straight days without getting lost.

"We don't need a map," Renaud insisted, back in our early days of travel.

He figured it was enough for him to drive the entire distance from Québec to Florida without expecting him to notice every little sign at the side of the road. Someone else (guess who?) should take note of, and interpret these signs. "It's the least you can do," he said. I don't understand why, after 20 years of me getting us lost while following the approximately same route south every year, he should assume that I can direct him without in-car visual aids.

How can I tell you
the right way to go,
and lead your path straight
every lap
If you must insist,
on coming unglued,
whenever I ask
for a map?

Not that I didn't appreciate his confidence in my powers of observation, but smiling jovially and saying, "Margie dear, you don't need maps, just watch the road signs," falls

69

far short of the mark when there are no roadside signs saying anything like "Yoo-Hoo, Florida straight ahead!"

I've tried to explain that there's no point watching for something as ambiguous as exit numbers, route numbers, highways, names of dead-ahead towns, etc., because without a map, those things mean nothing.

In our earlier travel days, before I-95, when there were fewer roads, less traffic and our nerves were in pretty good shape, we dealt with routes 17 and 301 as best we could -- maddening slowness, two-way traffic, alternates, and all.

But, of course, even then we made mistakes. For instance, at a fork in the road, without a map, how could I have known whether we would be better on 17 or Alt. 17? I mean, this was 'way back in 1953. And if it really didn't matter, then how come Renaud got so worked up about it after we drove for miles and miles along ocean highway Alt-17 and ended up paying, by the foot? And we were towing a trailer (yes, the red teardrop trailer), to cross the Chesapeake Bay on the ferry. And guess whose fault that was....

It's easier today with Interstates 81 and 95, and all the other direct arteries south, and beltways that by-pass or swoop over big cities, but even today's well-marked throughways aren't a sure thing.

Like the time I dozed off as we approached Syracuse and woke up to hear Renaud mutter, "...I don't believe it. I just drove past that building about an hour ago." We had gone straight through Syracuse, but at the south end of the city, Renaud wandered onto the beltway, northbound, taking us back to the same point where we had entered earlier

I suppose, in a way it was my fault, because I was dozing, but why should I take the blame when Renaud drives toward a sign screaming with 10-foot-high characters in glowing reflective paint, indicating some overgrown city that we wanted to avoid, and he heads straight into it like a bee heading for the hive.

Most of the time, I was awake, attentive and could spot trouble half a mile ahead, but I'll never forget the battle-fatigued, aching eyes that resulted the year of the mud-spattered windshield when the wiper didn't work on my side. The navigator's side!

It was like watching a tennis match through fly-paper as one sign after another loomed ahead, then zipped by while I tried to sort out the messages we needed from the messages we didn't need: Speed Limit, DETOUR, Slippery when wet, Wrong Way, Falling Rock Zone, Deer Crossing, Unmarked Patrol Cars, etc.

Throughout our travel years, in spite of good intentions, I continued getting us enmeshed in off-beat traffic snarls, in wrong lanes, in the few seconds it takes to glance through my purse for Life Savers or gum to unclench my rigid jaws.

Then there were those times I scrabbled in my purse for change for the toll road ahead and Renaud would yelp helpfully, "What do you mean you can't find the right change!? I'm *in* the Exact Change lane!"

Driving at night on strange roads was particularly challenging. We did a lot of that in the old days of two-way

71

highways, spending almost as much time getting lost and re-directed, as we did going in the right direction.

And we often ended up looking for accommodations in obscure little towns along narrow, poorly marked country roads, sometimes in a heavy rainfall. There's no more hopeless feeling than pushing doggedly ahead, with the in-laws in the back seat, while dark woods, slick pavements, sparse little towns and deserted gas stations waft past in the night – and no idea what's ahead or even if we're going in the right direction.

Renaud loathed being lost, and loathed even more the prospect of admitting it, and it's a real defeat to have to stop and ask for directions – which does nothing to elevate the mood at the onset of a desperately needed holiday. Strangely enough, we never became lost coming back home – just going away from home.

Then there are those pseudo patient stretches of silence. Like the time Renaud and I were being polite to each other because we became lost after breakfast, costing us half an hour of road time early in the day. I was indignant because I knew Renaud thought it was my fault, and maybe it was, but we knew that even before we got lost. In fact, we knew that before we left home, so what's the point?

We sat next to each other self-righteously, Renaud grim and silent, me contrite and silent. Folding my hands neatly on my lap, I coolly resolved not to make any comment beyond the call of duty, and even then only in the most reserved manner, when suddenly a sign looming toward us with alarming rapidity yanked me bolt upright with a terse howl of "Take this exit – now!"

With smoothness, precision and only minor squealing of tires, combined with a deft reconnaissance of the rear view mirror, Renaud spun out of the exit with the admirable calm reserved for people of his unfrayable nature – trusting his navigator to do the right thing.

Too late, I realized that the road number was right, but the small print under the number on the sign said: North.

The obvious solution was for me to have a Texaco road map laminated to fabric and made up into seat covers. But I never did....

Games of the Open Road

We seldom travelled alone. Sitting next to Renaud in an after-breakfast lethargy, feeling the warmth of the southern sun pelting through the windshield, I drifted in and out of a hazy ambiance of well-being. It was January 1969 and we were making good time, tooling smartly along the I-95 south of the Washington beltway, heading for Florida.

My head drooped and nodded to the car's gentle swoops and vibrations like a marigold, bobbing and swaying on its stem in a playful breeze.

Renaud's parents, Romé and Bella, dozed in the back seat, with our 8-year-old daughter, Linda, between them, also dozing. From the corner of a half-shut eye, I saw Renaud reach for a toothpick that he had earlier wedged into the door-frame moulding. Using it, he scratched gently at a tickle in his ear. I figured it was *his* ear, so said nothing. Suddenly, without warning, an arm descended from the back seat and delivered a resounding wallop to his elbow, jolting all of us upright, shaken and pale, as Bella scolded her son anxiously to, "Fais pas cà, Renaud. C'est dangereux!" Boy, it sure was dangerous. The shock alone could have sent us flying off into the ditch. Renaud managed to remain steady, luckily not having punctured his eardrum in reflex action. He peered cautiously around in disbelief, a plaintive "Ma-a-a-a...." his only comment. My heart, jerked from a relaxed state, responded to this incident with a wild banging.

Dramatic distractions in a moving vehicle are to be discouraged of course, but there's no doubt that, ordinarily, diversions breaking up the boredom of the long drive, are at least semi-welcome. Because, though "Stone walls do not a prison make, nor iron bars a cage," there's no denying the prison-like quality of being in a moving vehicle, all day, for three or more days with one's near and dear.

What could you do hour after hour sitting in a car? Twiddle thumbs, turn on radio, kick off shoes, adjust wearing apparel, change radio station, scratch an itch, examine run in nylons. A few tense minutes of navigating, then speculate on life in cosily illuminated, high-rise apartment buildings of a crowded city we're driving through, listen to argument in back seat when Romé and Bella can't agree on how long Uncle Zenon stayed out west when he took to the hills instead of following through on his intention of proposing marriage to his lady friend Fortunata.

74

An overturned truckload of chickens captured our attention, and so did a car being pulled over by police. So did a sign saying '49 miles to Pedro's.'

More restless fidgeting. Pass around Life Savers, referee an argument in the back seat about whose fault it is that Romé's cardigan button is missing. 'Welcome to South of the Border!' Study trees draped with Spanish moss. Stop for lunch. Pour a shot of cognac for Romé and watch Linda watch his expression as it goes down like bitter medicine. More tense navigating. 'Welcome to Georgia.' Listen to Bella complain when Romé coughs. "That's it, Romé, smoke. That's what makes you cough, you know." Remark on acrid, musty smell of swamps. Settle back, scratch again. Somewhere. Anywhere. On and on and on....

The first time Renaud's parents came south with us, in 1961, they had never been away from home in their lives (except on their honeymoon in the 1920s, which was a fishing trip up north with Romé's brother, Euclide, a dentist, and a doctor friend of his. Bella had waited patiently at the cabin while the men went fishing together. Yes, marriages were different then – and so were honeymoons). Now here they were, 38 years later, travelling all the way to Florida with us, and their granddaughter Linda.

This kind of dual-culture, intergenerational, thrown-together travel requires adjustment on the part of all participants. And we did adjust.

In St. Anicet, Romé and Bella's farm lay five miles down the road from us, next to our construction and farm equipment business. Romé was a tall, erect gentleman, who carried his slight frame with dignity, partly because of Caza pride, partly because he broke his collarbone in his 50s, locking him into a rigid carriage. He had fallen off a ladder at the barn. He had a tanned, hawk-like face, iron gray hair, blue-gray eyes, a kindly disposition and, in a friendly way, a gently argumentative nature.

Brought up in St. Anicet's old-fashioned farm community, he and Bella met while both families were picking wild strawberries in the fields near their homes. They married in St. Anicet's beautiful church (built in 1887) and raised a family of 8 children while farming tobacco and hops.

Romé developed (or inherited) a commanding, yet serene nature that put him in control whether he was right or wrong. Such as the night he went on the town with his brother Euclide. Horse and buggy days were long gone, but memory recaptured their essence after an evening of camaraderie, as they drove into the yard in Rome's blue DeSoto. He aimed toward the garage door between barn and house, braced both feet on the floor, gripped the steering wheel firmly, pulling it toward him, just as though good ol' Prince's and Maude's reins were in his hands, and called in a commanding voice "WWHHoooOOAAA!" as they crashed through the door.

He and Euclide stepped slowly from the car to survey the damage. Euclide shook his head thoughtfully. "Bella's not going to like this," he said. Romé wasn't worried. It was his car, and his door, and he was boss.

Romé was the sort of father who provided impossible advantages in hard times for his large family. He was also the sort of husband who liked his Bella to keep up with current trends and fashions, and wasn't above sending her from the car, back into the house before going to a Golden Ager's meeting if her cheeks were too pale to suit him. "Go put a bit of rouge on your cheeks, Bella," he would command gruffly. And she would comply.

Eight times a mother and 20 times a grandmother, Bella was a gentle, energetic lady with beautiful, soft brown eyes, abundant salt-and-pepper hair, comfortable, welcoming manner, and unparalleled patience. Her heart centered around the home, but she was a keen observer and interested in everything.

Romé and Bella were uncomplaining travel companions, even in those early years when our shoestring was thin and our car's defects ranged from the inconvenient to complete mechanical breakdown far from home.

There was the year of the stuck window on the driver's side so Renaud had to open the car door at the many toll booths, the year of the bum generator, the year that something smoldered under the hood every time we drove for more than a couple of hours at a stretch, sending up thick smoke in front of the windshield.

There was the year we patched the gas tank with softened soap from our motel, and used a paper clip as a shim for something under the hood. There was the year the gas gauge didn't register, the year the battery had to be boosted every single morning, and our night's motel selection hinged on the proximity of a service station.

There was also the year the gas line froze on our way home through the Adirondacks, and the year we were rear-ended in a blizzard between mountains at Dannemora on what was *supposed* to have been the last day on the road before home.

But old days or new, broke or solvent in our travels on old roads or new, there were the wonderful games of the open road. For instance, every year, at some time on our long road south, Renaud, thinking he was broad-minded and doing me a favour, would pull off onto the shoulder or at a rest area to allow me to take over as driver. Since he was an excellent driver, but an infuriating passenger, I didn't look forward to this privilege.

It was always the same story: as the time I replaced him as driver along a straight stretch of I-95, south of Brunswick, Georgia. Renaud parked, whisked around the car and slid in on the passenger side. I moved over and got behind the wheel. Renaud leaned back against the headrest, determined (he said) to get a few minutes of sleep. I fastened my seat belt and re-set the rear view and side mirrors.

"Now remember, Margie," Renaud said. "This isn't a road you're familiar with, so be careful."

"Uh huh," I agreed, pulling onto the highway.

"There's a car trying to pass you," Renaud said about a minute later, turning his head sleepily and peering out the rear window.

"I'm not trying to stop it, dear," I said.

"Well, just be careful."

"I will."

"Not so fast."

"Yes, dear." I slowed to 60.

Later, pulling out to overtake a slow-moving pick-up truck, I sensed Renaud tensing, though his eyes were closed.

"Why are you pulling to the left," he asked, trying to sound nonchalant.

"I'm passing a truck," I explained.

"A *truck*!" he exclaimed."Do you *have* to?"

I said "Yes." He opened his eyes, checked the situation, and accepted my decision to pass.

"Be careful, though," he said.

"I will."

Leaning back against the headrest again, he dozed fitfully for about 18 seconds.

"You're going too fast," he mumbled.

I slowed to 50.

"Too fast," said Renaud.

I slowed to 40.

"You'd better let me drive," Renaud said, suddenly sitting bolt upright, and directing me in for a landing on the broad paved shoulder. "You never know what darn fool's behind the wheel of those cars out there," he scolded.

Well, I wasn't about to argue with logic like that.

Then there's the gas game. The gas game was a bit of highway whimsy that proved boys will be boys, no matter how old they get. Sometimes known as, "*Let's-see-how-empty-we-can-get-the-gas-tank-before-we-stop-to-buy-gas*", this game undoubtedly came about because Renaud and his father are both Cazas more than as a means of relieving boredom on the road, because it doesn't happen when Renaud and I travel alone together.

Good for at least one performance per journey, each way, the gas game never changes:

"You'll need gas soon, Renaud," said Romé, perched on the edge of his seat behind the driver as we sailed past a nest of gas stations off the I-95.

"Uuummm," said Renaud, smiling unconcernedly.

Everyone peered at the gas gauge with the marker well below the ¼ mark. I sighed, Bella sighed, and Linda leaned toward my ear and whispered "Oh, good, they're at it again."

"Don't forget gas, Renaud," said Romé a little later, gripping the back of Renaud's headrest as we zipped past an exit that could easily have taken us to a gas station.

"Uuummm," he said, nodding agreeably.

As the needle edged toward flat empty, Romé leaned back stiffly in his seat and adjusted his cap over his eyes, folded his arms and declared that it didn't matter to him if we ran out of gas a hundred miles from nowhere and had to wait in the car while Renaud walked to a service station.

Meanwhile, Bella and I, apathy gone, furtively scanned the road ahead for the possibility of a gas station with a rest room.

Renaud smiled. "Don't worry, Pa," he said, "there's no danger of us running out of gas. I know what I'm doing."

"*I'm* not worried," said Romé

I leaned back, shut my eyes to watchful slits, and was overjoyed when, almost immediately, Renaud whisked through an exit into a service area accompanied, I'm convinced, by a faint sputtering as the engine sipped its last drops of fuel.

The Rest that Refreshes

"Well, well, well," said Renaud. He stretched and yawned as he unbent from the steering wheel while the attendant flowed gas into the dry tank. "While we're here, we might as well have lunch."

It was 1:30. We'd had breakfast at 7:00, so we were all famished. I yawned and stretched appreciatively. I unfastened my seat belt and turned to check that Linda and Bella were aware that we had just embarked on another road game as this normal travel necessity of refuelling merged into another popular travel pastime – Romé's *Gas Game Revenge*, known to us womenfolk as here-we-go-again.

Romé surfaced from his feigned sleep, looked around in surprise and exclaimed, "What! Time to eat again?" Adding succinctly, "I'm not really hungry at all."

"Well, maybe we should drive on for another couple of hundred miles, Pa," Renaud responded slyly, reaching for the door handle as though to shut it and be on our way.

"Aw, no, no. No, not on my account," protested Romé. Renaud paid for the gas and moved away from the gas bay to park at the Howard Johnson Restaurant parking.

He opened the car door and said, "Of course if you really aren't hungry, we can go on for another hour.... "

Romé protested. "If all of you are hungry," he said, "we'll go ahead and have lunch now. I don't mind. It's all right. It's just that I'm not really hungry."

"Well, Pa, don't worry about it," said Renaud. "You don't have to come in with us. You can stay in the car and wait if you like."

Bella, Linda and I weren't about to wait for a negotiated settlement and were out of the car, making fast tracks for the restaurant restrooms. We knew how the dialogue would go anyway, and it trailed after us in wisps as the men locked the car and followed us, arguing good-naturedly.

"Oh, it's all right," Romé said. "I guess I could go in with you. Maybe I'll even have a little bowl of soup. And perhaps a sandwich. Or a hamburger. Maybe some coffee. Yes, a cup of coffee would be good. And a piece of pie.... Pumpkin, if they have any."

In the '70s and '80s, travellers felt lucky because of the rapid development of split highways, beltways and smooth paved roads. All this meant safer driving and less travel time and time spent looking for places to eat. Service plazas sprang to life, providing gas, food and restrooms. Howard Johnson's and Hornes became famous overnight.

Before Howard Johnson's and Hornes, travellers had to search about in small towns for something to eat and were at the mercy of whatever they could find close to the highway. It was not always a delightful experience and our choices were often facilitated by eye-surfing contents of other diners' plates as we hurried along looking for empty tables or booths.

I have no doubt that I'm the most difficult person to please, either on the road south or in foreign venues. Having many food allergies, and a strong leaning toward plain fare, I have little inclination to be experimental. I don't even eat pasta, for heaven's sake, or donuts. Appearance and texture often guide my choices, and the only sauce I care for is the dressing on salads. So it's no surprise that clams and oysters are beyond the pale for me, and as for snails and their ilk, I have been steadfast in my stand that if you like them, more power to you, but I'm not ashamed to refuse to eat anything that crawled out from under a rock, no matter how scrumptious they're supposed to be when hot and buttered. While it's true that you don't know what you're missing if you have no basis of comparison, I'm willing to accept my limitations.

Those early years of domestic travel may have been a bit primitive, but they were fun. We set out prepared to enjoy all the challenges presented, and resignedly accepted such things as sticky tables, chairs and syrup jugs; brittle squares of icy butter that shattered into splinters or skidded off the plate to shoot to the floor or over to the next table when touched with a knife. There were jam pots with no spoons of their own, and with somebody else's toast crumbs on top (later replaced by jam filled plastic squares). Sugar dispensers and packets of sugar that spill as they're torn open were better than sugar bowls of the past. There were also such innovations as pouches of coffee cream that squirt when forced, pouches of syrup that splash or spill while trying to get that plastic cover peeled away, and crumbly crackers welded into casings that would confound Houdini.

Then there's the human element that provided us with mini-blunders that had us chortling, like when Romé, on our first journey south together, decided to order tea with his lunch. Loose tea in a little teapot was what he expected, so when he was given a little tea bag with string attached he tore it open and dumped it into his cup of hot water. "Cream or lemon?" asked the waitress. "Both" he declared, and proceeded to pour the cream into his tea, then added the lemon, with the natural curdling result.

Also pepping things up en-route were mealtime games. There was the one of naming all the states while waiting for our orders to come; naming countries of the world, and bodies of water. Or we might ask, if the house were on fire and you just had time to save three things – aside from human life – what would those three things be? Or if you were on a deserted island, what 5 books would you want to have with you? Or which one companion?

Always looking for variations on this theme, one day I asked my father-in-law, "If you could re-live any year of your life, what year would that be?" In an instant he turned to me with a gentle smile. "Next year," he said wistfully, "Next year."

∞∞∞

The most urgent part of the pause that refreshes is the restroom visit.

Anyone who thinks that restroom dramas are nothing to write about is either not paying attention, or they've never travelled with a Caza, because we attract a high rate of action in this area.

The first such incident I remember was Renaud's mistake when he entered a restroom while preoccupied with a business problem. He stood there, just inside the doorway, deep in thought, gazing absently at the washroom equipment. Then two nuns entered, bringing him quickly back to the present and out the door.

Then there was the time he ran from the men's room in a service area off the I-95, hurriedly rounded up Romé, Bella, Linda and me, from the souvenir shop, said, "The car. Quick, get to the car," and sped out ahead of us. There didn't seem to be a moment to lose, so unquestioningly we raced out the door after him, scrambled into the car, left with the squeal of tires, and were cruising along the highway with hearts thudding before Renaud told us what happened.

He explained that the stalls in the men's room were built about a foot from the floor. While he was in there, he glanced down and recognized a familiar pair of black casual shoes entering the next stall. Ah, Romé, he thought. Inspired by this rare opportunity, he decided to have a good laugh at his father's expense.

He waited quietly a few seconds for his neighbour to get suitably installed, then took careful aim, reached through the intervening space with his foot, made a forceful stamp on the familiar black shoe, and roared loudly.

The answering roar of outrage wasn't as familiar as the shoe, and definitely not the expected French expletive.

Renaud was as surprised as his unknown victim was, so he quickly said "Sorry," and made his escape.

I noticed early in my association with the Caza family that they never sat around stagnating. They were a nice bunch of people who heedlessly raced through life stirring things up. All I had to do was keep my eyes open, and sure enough, something would happen to transform an innocent situation into a knee-slapper.

Like when we stopped for lunch at a service center and Bella headed for the ladies' room. When she returned to our table, she was red-faced and laughing. She said she'd been surprised to open the restroom door and come face to face with a very familiar looking person all these miles away from home.

"I looked, stepped aside, nodded politely and said 'Bonjour, Madame'," said Bella. "And only then did I realize that I was greeting my own image in a full-length mirror."

Inattention also contributed to our misadventures, because Romé once saw Bella walk briskly through a doorway with MEN written above it in bold letters. Thinking fast he leaped to the rescue, hurried through the doorway, took her arm and proceeded to pull her out.

As he tugged one way and she the other, two girls pushed past him into the restroom. He paused, shook his head, backed out and looked up at the sign again. "M-E-N." No doubt about it.

Obviously these young girls weren't paying any more attention than his Bella was. Back he went, only to be pushed out again. That's when Renaud took note of the situation and pointed out to his father the full word "WOMEN" above the door. "Oooh," said Romé. "My mistake, I didn't see the WO, just the MEN."

Motels en Route

We had been told the best way to choose a clean comfortable motel is to pick a well-known chain, give your credit card number and reserve in advance. We never did that.

Our travel arrangements were more of the "Whichever way the wind blows" genre, highly contingent upon car breakdowns or getting lost, etc. Consequently, when we were ready to stop for the night, motel pickings were not only limited but all too predictable.

Because our winter holidays were short, hurried and poorly planned, the motels we stayed at ran all the way from a fresh carnation in a bud vase on the bureau and a striped peppermint on the pillow, to toilets that wouldn't flush, and a dead cockroach in the bathroom sink.

Since our aim was to cover as many miles as possible, we often decided after supper to drive for another hour or two before looking for a motel. We soon found that after-supper lethargy is no time to face streams of headlights on unfamiliar, and fast, night-time highways.

When our nerves were sufficiently frayed for us to admit we couldn't go another mile, we often ended up stopping at the first fleabag with a vacancy sign we came to, usually an upstairs room close to the highway, with a clear channel to throughway traffic noise.

Of course, we were always too tired to check the room first, and by the time we unloaded, locked the car, climbed the stairs, reached our room and found out what a great big stinker it was, we were not about to go back down to the office to complain, get our money refunded, load everything back into the car, and leave to find another "nightmare by the roadside." At that late hour, could we even find one?

We were not overly critical. A bad choice was not earth-shaking and we weren't greatly bothered by minor inconveniences, like no ice in the ice machine, or 2 drinking glasses for 4, 5 or 6 of us, or not enough towels. We were ultimate good sports, numbed by scores of bad experiences.

One thing that did matter was having train tracks 25 feet from the motel. Tracks that we hadn't noticed on check-in because it was too dark. This happened surprisingly often when we travelled the old 301 – which paralleled the North/South Railway tracks. Freight trains frequently jerked us awake as they trundled down the track, blowing their whistles for the level crossing around the bend, as we were attempting to drift off into exhausted sleep.

It was cause to speculate along the chicken and egg route: which came first, the motels or the railway crossings? Or the 301, for that matter.

∞∞∞∞

Motels improved, of course. So, perhaps, did we. As time went by, we were not as stretched financially and, edging toward the 1980s, motel surprises were more agreeable: water colours or oil paintings screwed fast to the walls, thick rugs, heavily-lined draperies on smooth-running tracks, lamps that really worked, remote control TV, and free-running toilet paper that didn't have to be pried off the roll.

As we got older, the travel industry became more interested in pleasing the traveller and began providing lots of fleecy towels, full ice buckets, coin-operated soft drink machines along carpeted corridors, honour bar, in-room coffee, and continental breakfasts in the lobby at checkout.

Early travels were made more memorable by not knowing until we moved in if the television worked or not, and if the bathroom door locked, or even shut all the way for that matter. With fellow live-ins who don't always check around to see if all are present and accounted for before heading to the shower, we learned to grab at towels quickly because once they've discovered the intrusion, instead of shutting the bathroom door quickly, they're prone to catch the occupant's eye and apologize. Today you can count on the quality of showerheads and motel beds but in our early days of travel, we were pretty sure that some motel-designer knot-head rashly decided that neither amenity had to be comfortable, thereby providing us with unwelcome highlights to our travels.

Some showerheads were totally inflexible and others so mobile they changed aim and force, depending upon water pressure from full in the face to mid-section to knees. Showers were often arranged, lettered or numbered so as to be a new learning experience at each motel – made worse if the lettering was small and you forgot to bring your glasses.

The befuddled traveller is not always up to the decision-making involved at the end of a travel-weary day.

While still in the bathroom, we can be grateful that the industry eventually did something about those green tinted bathroom mirrors that someone along the way considered to be a desirable flesh tone.

Surviving the hurdle of the bathroom, it was up to the bed to make or break the traveller's spirit. Cheap motels on old highways were predictably guilty and it was an exercise in futility to take that capricious old body away from home, wedge it into a car for 8 or 10 hours (or more), and expect it to drift off into restful slumber in a strange motel bed of unpredictable texture and resiliency.

We're talking about firmness you could tap dance on. Over the years, we have run the gamut of beds with springs so soft that Renaud and I piled together in the middle, like in a hammock, to springs so taut that I was afraid to sit suddenly on the edge for fear that Renaud might flip off the other side like a tiddly-wink and ricochet off the far wall.

But it wasn't always the motel's fault when travellers were more tired when they left the motel than when they checked in. Our friends John and Rachel and the couple they were travelling with stopped for supper. They then found a nice motel, unpacked and turned in at 9:30, intending to get up at 5:30 a.m. for an early start to the next day's travel. Their intentions were good but Rachel woke up during the night, looked at the clock and woke everyone up. They all went quietly through the mechanical early-morning paces of washing, brushing teeth, packing and closing suitcases. Then they loaded the car, climbed in and left.

They were well on their way when John complained, "Bastard! I feel more tired now than I did when we stopped last night." Only then did they look at the digital dashboard clock, to discover that what Rachel had seen as 5:00 on their analog travel clock – with the transposing of big hand and little hand – had actually been 25 past midnight. There's nothing like a good, 3-hour sleep after 10 hours driving to set vacationers up for a cheerless day.

As we became older and travelled more, motels improved, merging into a kind of tweed carpet, walnut veneer blur. But the most memorable motel rooms were those of the early days when money was so tight that it took real nerve to vacation at all. One accommodation in particular could have been a candidate for the 'Worst motel room in Florida' category in the Guinness Book of World Records. It was very late on a stormy night while we were travelling with Romé and Bella.

We had passed hundreds of motels with 'No Vacancy' signs leering out of the drenched darkness along a 2-way road paralleling the ocean. Suddenly, a 'Vacancy' sign loomed ahead. We stopped and, desperately tired, took the room, sight unseen.

The dirty little office should have warned us, but Renaud, shoulders sagging with fatigue and responsibility, paid for the room, picked up the key, and we drove down the hill in back to unit number lucky-7. As we opened the door of the room, we reeled. Stale air carrying the unmistakable mix of Lysol, mildew and mothballs, greeted us. It was too late to turn back, but our first glance (and smell) left us wondering if a night spent in the car would really be so bad. Hugging our raincoats tightly to us, we squeezed together in the doorway and looked numbly around.

The walls were bilious green, with brown trim. Scattered about on every flat surface were grubby seashells, intended, perhaps, to serve as ashtrays.

A chiffonier and dresser stood side by side against the far wall, with one of the two sagging double beds pushed up against their fronts so that the lower drawers couldn't be reached or opened at all, and the top drawers could only be reached and opened by crawling across the bed. Although, who cared, because we certainly weren't going to use them.

A lamp with a red corrugated paper shade stood askew on a fragile bedside table that had a broken leg splinted with half a shingle on either side, well wrapped with grocery string. It was obviously there just for effect, since there was no bulb in the socket.

Another lamp crouched on a rickety iron stand next to the bed by the door. I reached over and pulled the tasselled chain. It worked. There was also a single, low-wattage bare bulb stuck in the middle of the dark red, alligatored ceiling.

The floors were cracked and wrinkled red and green linoleum squares. These featured a lot of streaky black marks and general dirt, sealed in by generously applied coats of shiny, yellowed varnish.

Our rain-splattered shoulders slumped with disappointment. Or resignation. But we were there, and clearly, we couldn't back track. We looked at each other, and then moved gingerly about, hanging up coats and opening suitcases in tiptoe silence. Bella and I looked grimly at the narrowly separated beds.

Putty-coloured velour bedspreads, heavy with the dust of years of disillusioned travellers settled within their folds, drew us warily. As we jerked them back to assess the situation underneath, puffs of tan dust rose sluggishly in the cold, damp air, then re-settled.

Bella buttoned her sweater up to the neck, spread Romé's extra tee shirt over her pillow and said softly, "Well, I'm certainly not taking *my* shoes off!"

Bella and I looked apprehensively toward the bathroom door. We had no illusions left as we opened it and turned on the light. Even then, it took a moment or two standing in the open doorway to make sense of it.

Exposed pipes hung precariously out of the walls. And what walls they were. They were covered in bright, patent-shiny red oilcloth with great wrinkles and rips down all the corners. To complete the picture, cockroaches, stunned by the light, scampered into the darkness offered by cracks in the wall. A hot shower would have been welcome, but not here. Bella and I turned away. This was one time when "ladies first" was no favour.

There were no heaters or blankets, just the heavy velour spreads, so we crawled into the beds wearing most of our clothing. It seemed a prudent move on several counts.

I cringed down under the clammy, threadbare sheets, as close to Renaud as possible. We had just got used to the musty Lysol and mothball odour of the room, but now our weight and warmth on the mattress forced a fresh outpouring of the combination. It was small comfort to realize that somebody cared enough to dip the mattress in disinfectant.

Tired as we were, sleep did not come easily but, after a while, from the other bed I heard Bella sigh softly and Romé's customary snore. Renaud stirred carefully and muttered "Uh, boy...."

Shining past the too-short venetian blind, further offending my aching eyes, a glow of red and green neon blinked from up the hill in front of the office, flaunting its message through the rain sluicing down the dirty window.

'VACANCY,' it said, shining wetly into the dark night, reaching out to ensnare other exhausted travellers.

"Do you see that, Renaud?" I whispered, pressing closer.

"See what?" he mumbled sleepily.

"That sign out there," I said. "Apparently there are more of these rooms to rent." It was hard to believe.

To Fly or Not to Fly

It was 1970. January. Deep winter in St. Anicet. The water pipes were frozen. Again. Time to Escape Winter.

I have nothing against flying, and by nature I'm an optimistic person, but when Renaud called from the office that January day and said that we were going to Florida, I expected to start wedging things into the car trunk as usual. I halted in mid-mental stride when he said something about tickets.

"Uh, wait a minute," I said. "I think I missed something. What did you just say about tickets?"

"I said," he said in an even voice. "Call the travel agency and get tickets."

"What kind of tickets?" I asked quietly

"Plane tickets, of course," he said.

"Plane tickets?"

"Plane tickets," he said. "We can only take three weeks, so we'll have to fly instead of driving."

I was thrilled with the idea of a lovely, warm, unexpected holiday, but my first sentiments were more along the lines of our son Joey, who had once said of that mode of transport, and I repeated it now, "...in the air?"

Renaud said, "Of course in the air," and I agreed, even though everything in me leans toward keeping both feet on the ground.

Since that time, we've done a lot of flying. Renaud said logical, infuriatingly sensible things about statistics and 'Safer in the air than on those roads.' I concured, but the unease is there anyway. No one arrives at destination more surprised than I am and I immediately think that although fate has been kind, it will get us on the return trip.

So I always sat quietly on the plane, seat belt fastened, clutching a small bottle of Gravol, trying to look calm as I bargain with fate and promise that if we get through this journey, I'll become a perfect person in all aspects of my life. Finally, landing safe and sound, I am filled with such relief that, as soon as I get home, I kick off my shoes and sink back into being my old, imperfect self.

I'm less nervous these days. The seat belt stays fastened, but the Gravol is on stand-by rather than taken for granted. I'm astonished though at the degree of confidence most air travellers have. They accept the logic of flight as I accept the logic of baggy nylons. Granted, air travel means that instead of white-knuckling it along crowded highways for three days it can all be over (in a manner of speaking) in a few hours.

Eventually, I accepted flying as one of those insecure facts of life, but I will never be as blasé as those sweet, blue-haired ladies who, even when the 'Fasten Your Seat Belt' signs light up, and turbulence rocks the plane, head unconcernedly for the toilets, chatting gaily about "...a little rough today, eh?" as unexpected air pockets leave them laughing giddily and shrieking "Whoops..." when they hit the floor.

What's the attraction anyway for those mid-air visits to airplane toilets? One such toilet-bound exodus I witnessed caused such a traffic jam in the aisles of a packed 747 on a one hour flight from New York's Kennedy to Montreal's Dorval that the flight attendants chimed, "Forget the drinks, folks," and fielded ham and cheese on rye sandwiches even as we circled for our landing.

Since we had left a well-endowed airport less than an hour earlier, and were setting down at an equally civilized airport immediately, I had the good sense to stay attached to my seat through heavy cloud cover and severe bumps.

Over time, I gained enough confidence to stop examining the rivets on the wings and the action of the flaps. That left me time to look around and notice other things. Like the first-class section. But I read somewhere, long ago, that you must be very careful what you wish for, because you just might get it.

One way to get into first-class without paying extra for it is to have gone through an 'incident'. A potentially dangerous incident that bumps you to another flight, and up in class to make up for the inconvenience (of nearly dying).

One such incident was a hydraulics problem. We were with friends Ray and Germaine. It was their first flight, and we were going to Florida, "You'll love flying," I had exclaimed heartily on the way to the airport, as though I really believed it.

We'd had a toast and coffee breakfast at 7:00 and their son Richard drove us to the airport. For a change, because we were accompanied by another couple, we prudently reserved our rooms at Vito's Sapphire Sea Motel in Juno Beach. Vito would meet us at the Palm Beach airport.

But half an hour out of Montreal, the flight attendant announced "Nothing to worry about, but there's a change of flight plan. We have to land at New York's LaGuardia."

Approaching the runway, we looked out the window and saw a fleet of ambulances and fire trucks, "For us?" I asked Renaud.

Somebody mentionned the hydraulics, and somebody else said, "Does that mean the wheels won't go down?"

The first person then said, "No, they're down all right, but probably they just won't lock in."

We looked over at Ray and Germaine, who were looking interestedly out their window at the welcome committee on the tarmac. It was clear that they thought this was business as usual.

We did land safely, a new plane was readied, our luggage transferred, and we were settled in our upgraded first class seats, it was 2:00 p.m. And we were hungry.

There wasn't time to eat at the airport on the way to our new gate, and our new flight was lunchless. However, after a round of gin and tonics for Renaud and me, and Bloody Mary's for Ray and Germaine, we looked forward to landing in Atlanta and finding a snack bar.

But there wasn't time in Atlanta either, because we missed our connecting flight and had to arrange a transfer to another airline. Running to Delta check-in, we were given new boarding passes, then returned to Eastern for our luggage, then back to Delta to check it through. Then, a quick phone call to Vito to tell him about the delay.

We were a little wobbly by the time we boarded our Delta flight, again in first class, but this was not a meal flight either. To make matters worse, because we were in first class, our drink orders came in doubles. There were 2 Bloody Mary's each on Ray and Germaine's tray, and 2 Gin and Tonics each on our tray, and 8 bags of salted peanuts.

What was supposed to have been a 3½-hour flight was at the 12-hour point, and we'd had nothing but cocktails and peanuts since our toast and coffee at 7:00 a.m. Consequently we, who were used to drinks coming one at a time, and slowly, with our feet on the ground, were in the mood to greet the next arrival of doubles as the most hysterically funny thing ever.

Suddenly, Germaine surprised us by hauling a bunch of grapes from her carry-on bag. So we ate grapes and laughed and told jokes until we landed.

At Orlando, we called Vito again to tell him our new arrival time at Palm Beach International.

We landed in Palm Beach at 11:00 p.m. The airport restaurant was closed, and anyway, there was Vito, standing alone in the arrivals lobby. We greeted him heartily, followed him to the parking lot, scrambled into his car and headed north toward Juno Beach.

It was too late to rent a car, or buy supplies for our kitchenette, and the only consumable on hand was a duty free bottle Ray bought at the airport. So we settled in, had a nightcap, polished off the rest of the grapes and retired. We had flown first class - and I won't wish for that again.

Then there was the year, 1981, that Renaud and I went to England - part of an Avco planned business/pleasure/work holiday for 89 North American heavy-equipment dealers and their wives. The Canadian contingent was to merge with the U.S. contingent in New York, where we were to transfer to the overseas flight. However, in Montreal, we blew an engine shortly after take-off in a sudden snow squall, and caught fire. The lights in the cabin went off, and flames streamed along the starboard side widows. A passenger stood and called out, "Stay in your seats, keep your seat belts fastened," then sat down. There was no panic, just a stunned silence.

Our capable pilot turned the plane around and landed safely, and we made the 11:00 news that evening.

I didn't have so much as a wobble as I stood outside looking at the charred aircraft, but two of the women passengers refused to continue the flight with their husbands. I went numbly ahead and by the time the wobbles hit, we were half way across the Atlantic, and I was very glad to have a calm and comforting husband to hold my hand. That's almost better than a parachute...

Six is the Limit

The choice of travel companions should never be dictated by whimsy, launched on the tag ends of rural holiday merry-making. Especially when that whimsy leads to cramming 6 generous-sized adults, along with their winter boots and vacation luggage, into an 8-year-old clunker to set out on a 4-week, 1,600 mile test of the bonds of marriage and friendship.

It was 1964 and it all started with the usual Christmas at my parents' home in Guelph, Ontario, then New Year's at Renaud's parents' home in Cazaville, 6 miles down the road from where we lived.

Only 2 months earlier, chickenpox had swept through our household, striking down everybody, including me, but excluding Renaud who had the good sense to have had chickenpox when he was 7 years old. I just wasn't in the mood for it. Chickenpox, that is. Or Happy New Year-ing either, for that matter.

Time to think about a winter getaway. But it didn't start out to be a package deal. In fact, we were even anticipating getting back to the second-honeymoon stage of our travels because at New Year's, Renaud's parents announced that they would not be coming along to Florida with us this time. Mind you, we'd enjoyed their company on our southern journeys together, but it would be great to be alone with each other on vacation for the first time since our short red-trailer-to-Florida adventure, 11 years earlier.

We grinned shyly at each other, anticipating the carefree month ahead of sunshine and beaches. Renaud spent the last day making sure there were no loose ends at the business, while I prepared the kids, the animals and the house.

Over the next 24 hours, we delivered Billy and Joey to our friends Dorothy and Jules' place, 20 miles away in Valleyfield, Linda to Ray and Germaine's in Huntingdon, 15 miles in another direction; Happy, the dog, to the kennel and Putt-Putt, the cat, to the office.

Everything was going along smoothly, except that there was a winter blizzard. By the time we got home from delivering the children through the high winds and drifting snow, it was 10:00 p.m. and all I wanted was to pack for ourselves, straighten the house, get a hot shower and go to bed.

But Renaud said "Oh, come on," and persuaded me to accompany him to a party at the hotel in the village because "everybody's going to be there."

With a smile and a big embrace, he added, "After all, we're on vacation now."

I couldn't argue with that, so I changed into a plaid skirt and black pullover sweater and we put on our coats and trailed out to the car. I must have looked tired, because

Renaud tried to cheer me with another bear hug and, "It'll be good for you, honey." As we plunged between snow-drifts toward the car, he was reassuring. "We'll only stay a few minutes," he said.

I didn't believe him, but it wasn't easy to deter a Caza headed in the direction of a good time, and anyway, he was right - we *were* on vacation. Tomorrow, we would be Flori-da-bound. Alone. Together. Hold that thought. So couldn't I be a good sport now and accommodate my really won-derful husband in this tiny little demand on my time? Of course I could.

When we arrived at the party, good times were in full swing. Predictably, though, the few minutes expanded to 4 hours, most of which I spent mentally rummaging through my wardrobe to decide what to pack.

About 2:30 a.m., Renaud was talking animatedly with his brother Maurice, and the hotel owner, Albert.

Suddenly Maurice turned and darted across the dance floor, plucked his blonde wife, Marie-Ange, from her dance partner, and walked her back to the bar, head low, talking and waving his arms.

At that moment Renaud glanced my way, smiled win-ningly, and shouted "Margie dear, come here...."

A wave of apprehension flooded over me as I got up and walked toward him, a fixed smile on my face. I had an uneasy feeling that he was up to no good, and that another independent decision had been made à la Caza.

Renaud reached out, took my hands and announced that the substitutes had stepped in. We were still planning to leave within a matter of hours, but instead of going alone, or with Romé and Bella, we would be accompanied by brother Maurice and his wife. So much for a second honeymoon.

Maurice and Marie-Ange smiled happily, all shiny-eyed. Maurice threw a heavy arm over my shoulder, said "Sonofabitch, this calls for another beer," and Renaud said "Good idea." Maurice said, "Christ, Albert," to the hotel owner, "come and have a drink with us – we're going to Florida with Renaud and Margie."

Albert and his red-headed wife Simone, joined us, congratulating Maurice and Marie-Ange. They said, wistfully, how they hadn't had a real holiday in years, and they certainly would like to see Florida someday. So Renaud, naturally (for him), said, "Why not come with us?" They looked surprised and pleased and said, "Sure."

The spontaneity of rural people never fails to amaze me. Here we were, leaving for Florida in, for heaven's sake, less than 5 hours, and now two totally unprepared couples had accepted to come with us, with no arrangements made about their work, children, houses or packing, to leave home for a whole month.

Standing in the middle of the bar-room floor, stone cold sober and with three pleased-as-all-get-out men shaking hands, hugging and kissing everyone and congratulating themselves on the stroke of genius that led to this decision, I had nothing to offer.

Not that I minded the company. Maurice, Albert, Marie-Ange and Simone being good people, good sports and good fun, but I was mildly curious about who was going to ride strapped onto the roof of our old-enough, mid-size car. I smiled, I think, but I know the inner me was tight-lipped about the abandoned second honeymoon concept I had of this holiday.

I glanced questioningly at Renaud, who beamed delightedly at me, winked, leaned heavily on his brother, and exclaimed, "We should have thought of this before!"

By now, Marie-Ange and Simone realized that there were toothbrushes to pack and bathing suits to dig out of the attic, so we all peeled our men away from the bar and scattered to get things underway.

There was a lot on my mind. In fact, I was close to shock, but on the way home, I could think of nothing to say that would improve matters.

I looked over at Renaud anyway and said, "Renaud..." and he said, "Aw, you'll see, it'll be fun," and that was that.

Arriving at the house, Renaud sighed and drooped his shoulders in that way men adopt when they know they have to be defensive, slunk to the bedroom, crawled under the quilts, and lucky me got to do the packing. So much for, "...just a few minutes" at the party.

In the morning, Renaud wondered glumly over his fried egg, toast and coffee if Maurice, Albert and their wives actually intended going through with this holiday-for-6 -in-a-car-for-4, adding, "I'm sure they're all sound asleep and have no intention of coming with us. They just meant they'd *like* to come along."

I stacked the dishes, set the suitcases near the door and swept the floor while Renaud muddled about in the icy crawl space under the house to drain any pipes that hadn't yet frozen, so they wouldn't do so while we were away.

By 8:00 we were in the car and heading toward the hotel, where Albert and Simone were waiting, then to Maurice and Marie-Ange's, where, through the freezing gray, early dawn inertia shone a determination not to be left out.

While some things in life have nice, straight rules to follow, protecting innocents from unforeseen circumstances, poor judgment, sudden impulse and failing sanity, in the area of vacationing, whether to travel alone or by the half dozen is a matter of personal whim. The die was cast.

The Very Limit

Squeezing 6 fair-sized adults in winter coats and boots, along with their holiday luggage, handbags and a couple of 6-packs into our car took cooperation and outside help. Renaud's brother Yves, who came to see us off, had to stuff the last one into the car and force the door shut.

We all found that hysterically funny, and immediately our holiday shifted from last-minute preparations and uncertainties to the status of a rip-roaring good time.

In fact, from where I sat at the outset, squashed in the front seat between Renaud and Maurice, it looked like an extension of the partying of the past week. In other words, New Year's continued. Even accelerated.

We each eventually quit smoking, but back then doctors not only found little fault with smoking, they recommended their favourite brands in magazine ads.

Marie-Ange and I smoked cigarettes and the three men smoked cigars *and* cigarettes. Simone didn't smoke at all and, though she shouldn't have had to, she gamely breathed the smoke-filled air as we rolled along on the long, unwinding highway to Florida.

It's a good thing our lungs were young and resilient because the throughway pollution was nothing compared to the pollution inside the car.

The ashtrays overflowed and we sometimes had to pull off to the side of the road to scramble after cigars or cigarettes that, due to our tight squeeze, were jostled loose while still burning. And they had to be found.

It didn't take long for Renaud's mood to change from that of the New Year's camaraderie to one of, "Whose dumb idea was this anyway?" Since it was his dumb idea, he had no choice but to, in his very own words of the night before directed to me, "Be a good sport."

To make matters worse, I, with all home-related problems taken care of, and the chaos of the holiday season and departure preparations safely behind us, loosened up and became ally to the fun-seekers.

Renaud now found himself in the position of putting up with a car full of rowdy people. And there was nothing he could do about it.

We didn't get far that first day, due to late departure, stormy weather, exuberant passengers, and getting off the track a few times while trying to maintain our southbound orientation.

By late afternoon, we took a five-to-one vote to stop at Saranac Lake for the night. Renaud grumbled that with our late start (11:00 a.m. instead of the intended 7:00 a.m.), and the few miles covered, "We might as well have spent the night at home."

The rest of us applauded his wonderful sense of humour. We stopped for gas, and bought a 6-pack of tonic water. Then we checked into adjoining rooms at the Grand Union Motel.

After freshening up, our happy entourage walked to a nearby diner for supper, during the course of which Maurice left his cigarette burning in the ashtray, accidentally setting fire to a crumpled paper napkin while he crawled under the table of the booth to retrieve a button that Marie-Ange had lost from her blue sweater.

We put out the fire and unstuck Maurice from under the tight-fit table, then returned to the motel and 5 of us spent the better part of the night in high-spirited card playing. Renaud grimly refused to join in. He was the driver and very tired, threatening friendicide and worse if we didn't, "Cut out that noise!" and "Turn off those lights!" so he could get some sleep.

Maurice said, "Christ, we're on vacation," and "Sonofabitch, deal!"

In the morning, the card-players oozed dispiritedly out of the sack, dressed and stumbled into the motel restaurant for fortifying juice, coffee, eggs, bacon, and more coffee. Albert, eager to prove how hearty his appetite was, ordered and ate a second breakfast, and was promptly sick. It was 10:00 a.m. by the time we were back on the road.

For many irritating and some comical reasons, we only got as far as Washington the second night out. In the morning, we had debated hotly about whether or not we should take time to tour this historical city.

Renaud, cradling his head in his arms gripped around the steering wheel, protested grimly, saying that we were on our way to Florida, so we should at least try to get there, and "If you think I'm going to stop at every town along the way...."

Deciding in favour of the detour by a 5-to-1 vote, we arrived in Washington around noon, parked the car and hired a taxi (and if you think 6 in a car is a tight squeeze, try wedging all that in with a large taxi driver protesting, "But I can't *do* that!" We wouldn't listen.

We visited the White House, President Kennedy's eternal flame grave site in Arlington National Cemetery, and the Capitol Building, where we dissolved into helpless laughter because Marie-Ange told the Keeper of the Keys, who asked us where we were from, that we were Cazas, from Cazaville – a village of about 200 souls, 6 miles down the road from St. Anicet.

After we saw as much as we could see, the taxi driver drove us back to our car and, as if we weren't behind schedule enough already, we drove in circles for another 20 minutes before asking for directions. And guess what? It was time for supper.

Then, there were restroom stops – never frequent enough. To make matters more interesting, every time we pulled into a service station, the attendants froze in fascination as the car doors burst open to emit billows of thick, yellow smoke and at least 5 mighty quick people who boiled out of the car and surged toward the restrooms while Renaud raised the hood, checked the oil, checked the radiator, paid for the gas, and talked himself out of driving off and leaving all of us there.

By the third day, we made better travelling time, but my hair was stiff as a whiskbroom, looked like straw and smelled like cigars.

In Florida, we stopped at various touristy attractions along the roadside, including a helicopter-landing pad, where rides were offered. Marie Ange and Simone didn't hesitate, not even when they realized that there were no doors on the helicopter.

About 10:00 a.m. of the fifth day, we finally arrived in the Palm Beach area. We didn't have reservations of course. This launched us on a largely unproductive search along the ocean highway, laughing and joking with false heartiness about maybe having to spend the night on the beach, or in the car. Then we found an ancient, scraggly motel overlooking the ocean.

It was old and unkempt but we were past caring because we were learning that finding motel kitchenette units for 6 without reservations was like finding strawberries in a Canadian field in January.

Coasting into the parking lot, we pulled over in front of the office door where a grizzled, grey-haired, stubble-bearded man sat in a rocking chair on the pavement.

"Howdy," he growled as he heaved his stout self out of the chair and rolled toward us on ball-bearinged feet. His scowl would have discouraged less road-weary travellers, but it had been a long day, and it was worth a try.

III
BEING THERE

Charlie's Place

"Name's Charlie," he said. He was short, and sloppi-
ly dressed in faded everything. He had a pudgy face from
which peered pale beige eyes as sparkling as pork fat. As
we addressed him, another tough-looking, gray face poked
from a window, and then disappeared, to emerge through
the doorway seconds later, like a projectile. It was a woman,
with a stocky body and short legs.

She wore a wrinkled pink silk blouse, a pair of men's
brown work pants tied around the waist with a green neck-
tie. She also wore white ankle socks and a pair of black, Cu-
ban-heeled, Mary Jane shoes. Her hair stood out over her
head like a fluffy dandelion halo, gripped in the middle by
a yellow plastic butterfly barrette. We learned that she was
Charlie's sister, who helped him run the motel. Her name
was Lulu. And believe me, she was.

As they showed us around the suspiciously vacant
motel units, Charlie and Lulu alternated between holler-
ing at each other, "I told you, at least half a dozen times,
to get that toilet fixed," and at us, "What do you expect for
the price," and "You Canadians don't understand nawthin'
when it comes to money, do ya?"

The motel was pretty awful, but it did overlook the ocean, and the rooms adjoined with interior doors so we could leave them open and wander from one to the other without going outside.

There were two apartments, one with two double beds and the other with one double bed. There were two bathrooms, two refrigerators (one for food and one for the bar), two stoves, one that worked and one that didn't, and lots of tables, chairs, and seashell ashtrays.

We looked the place over, surprisingly not coming across any little brown hard-shelled bodies with heels kicking and antennae waving (they turned up later), and glanced questioningly at each other.

Seeing our indecision, Charlie turned taciturn. "What do you people want anyway?" he whined. Then, with a sneer, "What's the matter? Not lah-de-dah enough for you fancy people?"

Actually, Charlie's place wasn't lah-de-dah enough for a zoo, but considering the fact that we were 3 very tired couples, and travelling on a shoe-string budget, we were considering it.

Still, we had hoped to do better, so we said that we liked his place fine, but this was a group decision and we would have to discuss it among ourselves – over lunch. At the Howard Johnson's restaurant, just down the road. We would let him know.

We thought it over, meaning we skipped lunch and instead scoured the countryside for something better at a price we could manage.

Three hours later, hungry, cranky and willing to settle for what we could get, we sidled dejectedly back to Charlie's place, hoping that the apartments were still available. We needn't have worried. In view of what Charlie had to offer, nobody was standing in line. "Ha!" said Charlie, rising triumphantly from his rocking chair on the driveway. "I *knew* you'd be back!"

Digging into his pocket, he produced a tangle of keys, bit into his cigar, spitting the tip toward a pail by the office door, and glanced furtively around. Spotting Lulu at the clothesline, he urged us hurriedly toward Unit 1. In a hushed voice that conveyed conspiracy he said, "I want you folks to see something I didn't show you before."

Flinging the door of Unit 1 open, he preceded us over the threshold, tossed our key onto the bureau, paused dramatically and pointed straight in front of us to a partition separating the bedroom area from the kitchenette.

Set high into the partition was a large pane of frosted glass, about 2 feet square. On the frosted glass was painted a big pink rose.

Charlie swaggered over to the wall, said "Jus' look at this," and flipped a light switch. We all gazed speechless as the rose bloomed into full colour, shining down in a vulgar pink glow on the double bed.

Eyes misty, Charlie stretched up on tiptoe and puffed out his chest. "Made it myself!" he bragged. Appearances can be deceiving. Charlie was a romantic at heart, "Ain't it purty?" he said, chewing his cigar and rocking gently to and fro.

"Sonofabitch, it sure is," said Maurice agreeably.

The rest of us, dumbfounded, said nothing. I wondered which lucky couple would end up in the cupid suite. In the end, we alternated weeks.

Charlie no sooner left than Lulu stamped into the room carrying sheets and towels over her arm. "You'll have to clear out of here if you want me to get these rooms made up," she said grimly.

We thought they were made up, but since I had just opened a bureau drawer and discovered a cockroach factory, I was eager to accommodate and headed for the door.

"I have to do everything around here," Lulu announced as we hurried over the threshold. "Run, run, run, that's all I do all day long. Him," jerking her thumb toward Charlie, once again serenely imbedded in the rocking chair out front on the pavement, "He's no help. Just stands around gabbin' all day long. Never lifts a finger!"

She flung sheets and towels on the table, wrenched the bedspread off the first bed, then stood, fists on hips, glaring at us as we scurried away.

∞∞∞∞

We headed south to escape Canada's winter and, while escaping, we were determined to experience everything we could cram into our southern sojourn; Cape Canaveral, Citrus Tower, Cypress Gardens, Parrot Jungle, Key West, dog races, horse races, Jai Alai, flamingos, citrus on the trees, coconuts hanging in their thick casings, ocean waves, alligators in the everglades, air-boats, and especially that helicopter ride for Marie Ange and Simone.

114

With no television, our days became a jumble of card-playing, sightseeing, staying up late, sleeping in late, sunburns and assorted adventures – like Marie-Ange almost getting swept out to sea when caught in the edge of a riptide.

Sometimes we ate in restaurants, but most of our meals were can-opener inspired, primarily franks and beans. Housekeeping was light and done quickly with personal laundry done by hand and hung on Lulu's clothesline down the hill in back.

Nearing the end of the first week, we looked forward to fresh bed linens and towels. What with sea, sand and heat, we certainly needed clean ones. But, as week two began, there was still no sign of a housekeeper's trolley. Gathering our forces, we three women went to confront Lulu in her apartment.

As spokesperson for the group, I laughed lightly to show Lulu that there were no hard feelings. "Did you forget us?" I asked. "We don't have our clean sheets and towels."

Immediately, I realized that we were overstepping, because even as I finished my little speech, Lulu sprang up on her black Mary Janes, very nearly keeling over, and shrieked indignantly, "What do you mean, clean sheets? You mean you expect to have your laundry done for you? At the rates you pay? Now see here..." She wiped her hands on the apron sheathing her solid stomach and glared at us, quivering with outrage.

"We're not some fancy, high-priced Ho-tel you know!" said Lulu. "What do you expect when you pay rates like this? Maid service? You got dirty sheets? Fine! That's *your* problem. You're the ones got 'em dirty. *You* wash 'em!"

In some alarm, we backed out the door as Lulu advanced, brandishing a vacuum cleaner nozzle. She continued her tirade. "I got enough to do around here without running no fancy laundry service for no rich tourists. I do all my own washing, don't never send nothin' out. Think I can keep up with every Tom, Dick an' Harry wants to have clean sheets every five minutes? Ha!"

Charmed as we were to be upgraded to the classification of rich tourists, it began to look ominously as though we might be forced to the washboard at vacuum cleaner nozzle point.

Like cowards, we scurried back to re-examine the offending sheets. They were so fragile, it was doubtful they could survive washing. Marie-Ange was the most discouraged because their sheets were the thinnest, most patched and worn ones of the lot, and their top sheet had a long rip down the middle. Now, with all hope of fresh sheets gone, it was up to us to deal with the problem.

Marie-Ange got out her sewing kit and Simone and I sat with her as she tearfully mended the worst sheet while telling us what she thought of Lulu's austerity measures.

From then on, it was a delicate balance between the worn out linens and how much washing they could take. Even by hand. By the time our holiday at Charlie and Lulu's place was finished, the sheets weren't far behind.

Holiday over, we packed our bags and were loading the trunk of the car when Charlie came to say good-bye.

Lulu plunged ahead of him, darted into the apartments and looked about sharply, perhaps to make sure we weren't walking off with her precious bed sheets or dreadful sea-shell ashtrays.

That's when she noticed two brown paper bags of garbage standing just inside the doorway.

"Now you people see here!" she shrilled. "You take that garbage out!"

Maurice, mid-way between motel room door and car, stuffed his hands in his pockets, glanced at Lulu in surprise, and said "Christ, what do you want us to do, take it with us?"

Lulu advanced on him with a withering look, and the battle was on.

"Get that garbage out of here," she shrieked, picking up one of the brown bags and thrusting it at Maurice's chest. A few fish bones and an empty tonic bottle fell to the ground. Maurice took his hands out of his pockets and grasped the bag before it landed on his shoes. Lulu cupped his elbows in her palms, turned him around, and propelled him a few feet to the driveway, toward the hill behind the office.

She picked up the second bag and launched it at Albert. "You two carry those bags down there and put them in one of them big garbage bins. Go on now, git!" Renaud paused in wiping off the car windshield to see what was going on. Albert put his arms around the bag of garbage, and headed toward the hill.

Maurice stopped and looked sideways at Lulu. Clearly, he was trying to decide whether or not to flatten her. Chivalry won, however, and he carried the bag along the driveway, setting it in front of the office. Albert followed. Lulu wasn't about to settle for partial victory however. "What's the idea?" she screamed. "Don't you think I've got enough to do around here without running and carrying your garbage for you?" She stomped over to Maurice and declared, "This here is *your* garbage. Put it in back there. In the cans down the hill like I told you. Go on now, git!"

Standing off to the side, Charlie was obviously enjoying this contest of wills. Hands in pockets, he grinned, puffed on his cigar and rocked back and forth on his heels.

Marie-Ange, Simone and I watched too, speechless, and in definite awe of any woman who could talk to our men like that, and get away with it. We wondered if Lulu would win, and may even have been rooting for her. I mean, we didn't think she was right in her approach, but we admired her courage.

Our heads swung back and forth as the advantage passed from one to the other. Finally, the men picked up the bags and headed for the hill.

"Christ," muttered Maurice later, wiping his hands on a paper towel, "She could have asked nice." And, "Sonofabitch, did you ever see such characters as those two?" I made no comment, but hoped nobody was watching and thinking the same thing about us.

∞∞∞∞

Heading north, we decided to see the west coast of Florida and en route drove past thousands of acres of orange groves, and dozens of fruit stands. Until we were safely out of the state, Renaud's sole contribution to the conversations had to do with discouraging everyone from adding to the weight in the car by buying citrus, pecans and souvenirs from the roadside stands to take home.

Aside from that, the trip home was the usual scramble until, on the last day, our car's generator petered out over the Keene Mountains during a terrifying winter blizzard, leaving us with little power, dim headlights, scared passengers and not a hope in the world of getting out of this one alive. Until we coasted down a hill, rounded a curve in the snow-shrouded forest, and a tiny, dimly lit wayside gas-station-snack-bar appeared, to provide almost warm coffee, a filthy, dirty rest room, and blessed refuge from the storm while awaiting repairs.

Vito's Place

It was 1973. Linda was 13 years old. It was also Romé and Bella's 11th winter holiday south with us.

Ben and Marie, Stanley and Dot, Frank and Kathleen, Ira and Mary – the familiar regular winter tenants, wandered up from the beach and out of their apartments to welcome us back as we oozed out of the car to stretch in the sunshine after our 3-day drive. Vito came out of the house and walked toward us thoughtfully.

"Ah, you gots Linda wit' you again," he growled, smiling at us and reaching out to embrace her and shake hands all around, He looked at the 5 of us thoughtfully, said, "You should'a call. We pretty full up."

He paced back and forth a few times, and then smiled. "Well, we jus' finish paint unit l," he said. "Peoples is comin' in end of week, but can let you have four days. Then you have apartment under house for week, in uset'a be garage. Then we'll's see what we's can do after that. How long you stayin' this time?"

Penny waved as she drove in front of No 4 with her groceries, and Linda hurried past the coconut palms to the beach. It was good to be back. Good to see our old friends. Vito handed us our key and promised that our room would be ready by 3:00. We wandered to the bluff above the ocean and watched Linda chase the waves and flap her arms at the sea gulls.

"Let's go to lunch," said Renaud, drawing a finger across the winter road salt bloom along the side of the car. "Then we'll stop at that new car wash we passed a couple of miles back."

At the car wash after lunch, a freshly washed and waxed car was still standing on the triggering device while the driver opened his window to polish his outside rear-view mirror.

Without thinking, Renaud dropped the coins in the box, activating the spray trigger and water shot through the window of the car ahead of us. The driver rolled up his window, turned to give us a despairing look, and drove off. The car full of Cazas had, however unintentionally, done it again. On to Winn-Dixie to buy groceries.

Our apartment was ready when we arrived back at Vito's. We stepped over the threshold one at a time, setting down grocery bags and luggage as we looked around. It was the same room we usually had. The same furniture. But it had been painted. It was now all white. A white so dazzling that we squinted.

The pale gray terrazzo floor and pale gray table and chairs were the only things that weren't white. Draperies, lamps, walls, ceilings, towels, bedspreads, everything white.

Equally startling were 4 twin beds and a camp cot lined up shoulder to shoulder in white chenille shrouds, exactly like a dormitory. Or a hospital ward.

Still laughing, Bella and I put away groceries while the men created more space by shoving the 4 twin beds together to make 2 double beds, and moving Linda's camp cot into the walk-in closet. It was still crowded, but at least we were settled in.

The next morning, I awoke to the sound of waves slapping on the beach. I reached over and picked up the travel clock. Seven. I looked around at all the beds and the sleeping forms of Renaud, Bella and Romé, and at Linda's feet sticking out of the walk-in closet.

I drew on my housecoat, tiptoed to the door, slipped out quietly and walked to the beach over the soft sand path angling down the bluff. A flight of pelicans passed overhead. Gulls screeched, and sandpipers picked busily at bubbles left by receding waves.

I brushed sand off the wooden bench pushed against the bottom of the bluff, just above the tide line, and sat down. A bossy-looking puffed-up politician seagull, protecting his stretch of beach, screamed at the intrusion.

Ahhhh, back again. It was lovely to watch the rhythmic ocean waves wash up on the beach at my favourite, quiet time of day, with three more weeks of it ahead.

Instead of ice and winter blizzards, framed by my St. Anicet kitchen window, smoky green swells flattened smoothly, fanning out like paint from the sweep of an artist's brush onto the textured palette of hard, ivory sand.

Lifting higher, the sun charged the cool dawn air with humid warmth. Surf pounded in prescribed travelogue manner, and palms rasped like gentle, rhythmic sandpaper.

I felt downright sappy with sentiment, and exuberant with a rush of well-being. I caught a movement to my right and looked up. Renaud, wearing light summer slacks and tee shirt, creased from packing. He needed a shave, but the smile on his face was not the smile of a harried construction man; it was the smile of the man I married that November morning so many years ago in St. Anicet. He sat next to me, took my hand, and together we watched the sea and gulls. It was time to coast into the happy annual adjustment.

Mornings at home we bounded out of bed to face another day of jangling telephone calls and demands of business, home and family, but in Florida we could open one eye, turn over and go back to sleep. Or rise early, like now, and enjoy the sunrise. There's time for a morning hug and kiss, a leisurely stretch and yawn, and a shared day ahead.

It took time for us to get used to the shifts in gears book-ending our vacations. First, bracing ourselves for the happy rush of escaping winter, then dealing with the idea of ho-hum, back-in-the-rut routine as we headed back north.

Ah, I thought, now he's mine again, this husband who has glowered and looked harassed all year. For the whole month, we will run together along the sandy beach, and play in the pounding surf, forgetting all but maintaining our balance and being wonderfully together. Proving once again that, through all the summer months of business, work and responsibility, this annual renewal sustains a harmonious relationship. A relationship that had merely, in fact, been relegated, like so much rutabaga, to the root cellar of making-a-living, for a general ripening, to be looked at anew by the grace of a winter vacation.

I'm delighted, of course, and bask happily in all this affectionate attention, even though I know that the moment we get back home, Renaud's worried frown will return and I'll be dropped like a brick in favour of more urgent stuff, like camshafts, radiators, hydraulic dumps, broken grader blades, shovel teeth, drag-line cables, and income tax. But for now, ah, enjoy, enjoy...

Things that go "Weerroooo" in the Night

The logistics of 5 people living in a small, one-room motel apartment called for adjustment and agility. After 4 days of bumping into each other and falling over furniture, we looked forward to moving into the larger (although darker and less airy) converted garage apartment – with separate bedrooms and an extra bathroom.

Our suitcases were ready to take the short trip down the hill to the larger apartment when Vito came to tell us we could stay where we were because he rented the renovated ex-garage to someone else. He justified his action by saying that the people he expected to take the room we were in, called and cancelled, and he assumed we would rather stay where we were than move. He was wrong, of course, because we would have preferred the extra bedroom in the converted garage, but the deed was done.

So we were reinstated in our crowded five-in-a-dorm-room situation and continued membership in the Barked Shins Club, and for the rest of our stay at Vito's, we cursed the low foot-boards on our rank of beds that turned our motel room into a minefield. Whenever a Caza turned around or moved quickly, he/she was ambushed by the furnishings.

The sharp-cornered footboards, just rising to mid-shin height, and disguised by the soft white chenille bedspreads, caused more black and blue distress among our close-pressed group than boxing night at the Forum.

What's more, it wasn't unusual to have several consecutive shin 'barkings', and even simultaneous ones when we were all milling about. This pain parade merged with toe-stubbings, resulting from meanderings around the 6 solid wooden feet that belonged to each bed.

It was not uncommon to be awakened at night by a jolting shudder of the bed and muffled curses as some hapless victim made footboard-to-shin or toe-to-wooden-foot contact on the way to or from the bathroom.

Bed footboards and feet weren't the only hazard of our cramped quarters. There was also the sharp-edged cupboard between dining area and kitchenette, the rocking chair whose arms got up when the sitter did, and the other rocking chair that, if rocked back just a little too far, did a complete back flip, dumping the occupant.

Dark-of-night hazards were the most challenging. And memorable – like the rabbit-ears antennae on top of the old portable TV that sat on a stand between the walk-in closet and the bathroom, whipping out at passers-by like an épée.

We were into our second week of booby-trapped motel living when the wind came up suddenly during the evening. Rain sluiced softly, "Pluuitt-Pluuuittt..." against the big windows facing the ocean. It didn't matter. It wasn't snow. I knew the sun would shine the next day, and it was cozy sitting around the room, each of us absorbed in our little relaxations.

I finished my cup of tea and listened while Romé, Bella and Renaud talked about Uncle Zenon, Aunt Cecile, Euclide, and the good old days. Linda worked on a scrapbook about her Florida vacation, then took out her school homework. One by one, we called it a day, taking turns at the bathroom.

By the time I had my shower and tiptoed back to the dorm, all was quiet. Palms swished in the wind, and rain splatted firmly against the windows as I settled snugly into bed, listening to the surf pounding rhythmically on the beach a few yards from the window near my pillow. I was just drifting off when Renaud stirred, sighed, drew back the covers, winced as his bare feet touched cold terrazzo floor, and got up to grope his way to the bathroom.

Tiptoeing in the dark so he wouldn't wake anyone, going slowly so he wouldn't smash his shins against the footboards, arms raised high and outstretched in front of him so he wouldn't crash into the open door of the walk-in closet that had been left open to make room for Linda's cot, he made his careful way to the bathroom. Suddenly there was a muffled howl, followed by a soft curse.

"The footboards?" I asked sympathetically when he finally slid back into bed next to me.

"No, dammit!" he said, snuggling close and pulling the covers up.

"What happened then?" I asked.

"You know the TV?" he growled quietly into my ear.

"Hummmm," I acknowledged.

"Well," he said, "I was moving carefully, my arms high and stretched out so I wouldn't bump into the door and, you know the rabbit-ears antennae?"

"Hummmm," said I.

"Well, it got me right in the armpit."

Then, there was the midnight haunting. Distant but becoming more pronounced, a high-pitched wailing woke us all to nape-of-the-neck prickling alertness one windy night.

It faded, then again rose in volume. Louder, higher, more penetrating and no longer in the background. No longer a wail either, but a penetrating screech.

"WeerrOOOWWRRROOoooooo," it howled.

"Wasssat," grumbled Romé from the other bed.

"The window in the back door," mumbled Renaud sleepily. "It's loose. The wind must be forcing through it."

After several more loud howls as the wind rushed through the crack between window and door frame, we were all sitting up in our beds. I turned on the table lamp. Linda looked owlishly around the corner of the closet. Renaud poked at the frame around the window, and the noise stopped. He came back to bed. I turned off the light.

No sooner were we settled back on our pillows than the howl took off like a frenzied factory whistle.

By this time, and no matter how funny it seemed to Linda, Bella and me, it was clear that Renaud was getting to the end of his rope.

He approached the door grimly, looking for, if not a cure, at least someone to blame it on. "Did you do something to the door when you locked up?" he asked crossly. He didn't really expect an answer and he didn't get one, so he sat on a chair by the door and studied it intently. He lit a cigar and waited. Not a sound. Satisfied, he put out his cigar, turned off the light, and climbed into bed. Sure enough, "WeerrOOWWRROOooooooo," it howled, as Linda, Bella and I collapsed in giggles.

The rain sounded louder; surf crashed and palm trees on the patio thrashed about wildly, but over it all, the haunted door triumphed. "WeerrOOWWWRRROOoooooo." It was too much for Romé, who had been watching the whole drama silently from his bed. He jumped up and padded over the cold terrazzo floor to the door in his pale blue boxer shorts and white T-shirt, hair standing on end. He picked up a cigar box, tore off a piece of the flap and wedged it into the space between window and door frame.

"There!" he declared. "You just have to know how to do it!" He went back to bed, I turned out the light, and there was silence. For about 4 minutes.

"WeerrOOWWRRRooooo." it howled again.

Renaud and Romé went back to the door, but no matter how they fiddled with cardboard shims, kicks and threats the haunting continued intermittently until the wind died down – much later.

It wasn't easy to settle into sound sleep on vacation. Even at Vito's, where we were more or less at home. The mattress was different, night noises were different, branches scratched at the walls and, soon after dawn arrived, slippered feet padded past our door on the way to an early ocean swim, and fishermen clattered by eagerly and loudly, discussing tackle on their way to the beach. Newspapers thunked on one doorstep after another the length of the motel, seagulls quarrelled, a garbage truck clanked.

Here we were in Florida, on holiday, where we could lie in bed as long as we wanted, and all these annoying noises kept us awake. The stark brightness of our room in daylight was no help either. With all the early morning sounds, white curtains and no window shades to darken our white room, it was like trying to sleep in a well-lit factory.

I opened my eyes and listened to the ocean noises. A faint voice called. It was a voice I had heard another morning, too. "Barrr-nnarrrrd," it pleaded querulously. I glanced over at the travel clock. 6:30. What was that noise? "Barr-nnarrrd," it insisted closer now.

Bella stirred. Romé and Renaud snored softly. Linda, curled up in the walk-in closet, got up sleepily and padded to the bathroom. The voice persisted "Barrr-nnarrrrd, Barrr-nnnarrrd." It was near our door now. Bella muttered, threw her bed covers aside, reached for her robe and got up.

"There's no Bernard here, child," she muttered softly, anticipating that she would be confronting a youngster looking for a friend outside. "Go look for your little friend someplace else and let us sleep."

She opened the door and for a moment stood motionless and silent. Then she said "Shoooo, shoooo," shut the door and went back to bed.

Curious, I sat up and looked at Bella. She looked back at me, shaking with quiet laughter, her face flushed.

"Its a cat," she said. I got the full translation from Renaud at breakfast: "A great, big, marmalade cat. I opened the door in mid-yowl expecting to see a child looking for his friend, and there he was, sitting there looking up at me – just like a dog baying at the moon. He looked almost embarrassed as he turned and slunk away into the hibiscus. "

Home Away from Home

Bella wanted grapefruit. "I want pamplemousse," she told the man at TerMarch's fruit stand, south of Vito's.

"Yes, ma'am," he said, smiling and pointing sweepingly toward several crates of fruit. "Some of those?"

"Yes," said Bella, smiling trustingly, then headed for the honey and marmalade shelf.

When we were back at Vito's, she opened the paper bag to find, not grapefruit, but oranges.

"Oranges!" exclaimed Bella. "But I asked for pample-mousse..."

"Well, he gave you oranges," said Renaud.

"Exactly what did you ask for?" I asked suspiciously.

"Pamplemousse, I asked for pample-mouss!"

"I know," I said. "But did you say 'grapefruit' or did you ask in French?"

"I asked for pamplemousse."

"Uuummm... well, he didn't understand that pample-mousse is grapefruit in French," I said. "He must have thought you were pointing toward a particular type of orange. It might have been better to ask for grapefruit."

"Well, I know grape," said Bella, "...that's a small purple or green fruit in bunches – raisins. I didn't want raisins – I wanted pamplemousse."

Linda found some words unfamiliar too. "You should see the hot biscuits on the bushes this morning Mom," she said, running into the room and pulling me out on the patio. Truly, the blooms on the hibiscus were beautiful.

Admittedly, language snafus added a bit of spice to the vacation, but an old black and white television set with three English-only channels made entertainment sparse for all of us. In nice weather, we went for walks, or sightseeing, but rainy days and long evenings were often spent playing cards and story-telling, à la Caza... "Did Ma ever tell you about the $40?" Renaud asked me one evening. She hadn't, so I settled back for a cozy listen.

130

Bella, like all St. Anicet farm wives of her generation, always tucked a little egg money away in a safe place for emergencies, like gift shopping.

Bella's nest egg was $40, 2-$20s, folded just so. But she worried about it and was forever changing the hiding place.

One day, she went too far, hiding it so well that she couldn't find it. Then she drove herself, and everyone else in the family, to distraction with her searching. She looked under rugs, in the sewing machine drawers, in old purses and shoeboxes. Eventually she decided that a wanderer must have come into the house and stolen it. An unthinkable possibility, but no more unthinkable than a new suspicion she might have hidden it in another favourite hiding place – in a box of tissues on her bureau. The tissue box had since been burned in the kitchen wood stove.

"Forty dollars is a lot of money," said Bella. "I couldn't accept that someone passing by might have come into my home and found and stolen it. And I couldn't forgive myself if I thought I might have burned it accidentally with the tissue box. I needed to find that money.

"Mes cher amis, it was awful," interrupted Romé, shaking his head at the memory. "She lay in bed at night sighing and tossing, wondering out loud about what might have happened to it. And every once in a while she'd get out of bed and look in a new place she'd just thought of – or even old places that she'd already checked many times."

"During the day, while tending to household chores, she had a far-away, distracted look in her eyes," he continued. "It was the only thing on her mind. All we did was look for those two $20 bills, folded just so, not too worn and not too new. She had big plans for that money."

Renaud said, "It wasn't safe to step into the house. She made us move all the furniture in every room. Several times. It was clear that there would be no peace for anyone if she didn't find the money. She was making herself sick and everyone else was reluctant to come to the house to visit."

"Did you ever find it?" I asked. There was a moment's pause as a distant, puzzled look came over Bella's face.

"Well, yes," she said. "Yes – I found it..."

There was another, thoughtful silence. Renaud and his father exchanged a conspiratorial wink. I looked curiously at their flushed faces, and then turned to Bella.

"Well," I asked impatiently. "Where was it?"

"Actually," said Bella. "It's Romé who found it."

"Well, that's wonderful," I said, "...where?"

"Yes," said Bella, absently. "But I don't understand it. If there's one place I can't ever imagine myself hiding money it would be in the pocket of a pair of Romé's pants. I mean, why would I do that?"

One look at the men's faces and the cat was out of the bag. "Bella," said Romé, gently. "You burned the money in the tissue box. We were all sure you had, but you wouldn't accept it, and you wouldn't rest until you found it, so there was only one thing to do."

"Pa took two $20 bills from his wallet," said Renaud. "Carefully folded them according to the description he'd heard so often, and pretended that he had just found them in the pocket of his old pants hanging on a hook in the closet. He knew he would have to say he found them some place she hadn't already looked, and the only place that she wouldn't have looked would have been somewhere she wouldn't have put it – her husband's clothing. So the money was 'found' and peace restored."

As the story unfolded, Bella, touched that he had been so generous and so concerned, wiped tears from her eyes and gave her husband a grateful hug and kiss.

That would appear to be the end of the story, but when we returned home from Florida, Bella started spring-cleaning. She pulled out the bureau drawers to dust the guide channels (yes, she was a meticulous housekeeper), and there found, stuck in the runner, her $40. She must have stuffed it hastily into the drawer and it migrated down to the guides.

Later, on Romé's birthday, with the whole family gathered around the supper table, he opened a birthday card on his dinner plate and withdrew from it $80. To replace the $40 he had hidden in his pants pocket for Bella to find, and the original "lost" $40. Thoughtfulness rewarded – with interest – and another hug and kiss.

I loved the stories. When the sun went down, or it rained, or was too cool to be outside, there were stories. Stories liberally sprinkled with family anecdotes and larded with disagreements about Uncle Zenon's travels, and questions of: which cousin married a Murphy; about Aldea, Merilda, Rhéa, Valeda, Juliette and Cecile (Romé's sisters), and his brothers, Edmond and Euclide. About Meline and Albina, and Salome (who was a nun); about Theophile, Alexina and Aime; and about Alexis, who was mayor of St. Anicet several generations back, and who was called "North-Star" because he was so tall (6'7"). About Jean-Baptiste Lebeau-dit-Caza, who married in St. Anicet in 1822, who was the son of Pierre Lebeau, who was the son of Etienne Lebeau, who travelled from France and docked somewhere near Québec City in the late 1600s.

Other times, we played cards in the evening. With Bella and Romé as partners, it was always the same scenario. "Bella, why did you play the second bar on my first?"

"It was the only trump card I had left!" said Bella, "and I had to play trump."

"Well, why didn't you play it when I played the ace?"

"Because I knew you would take that hand with the ace. I waited for you to come back with a smaller card for me to take it. After all, I *did* bid hearts, too! you know!"

Romé would have preferred to play both hands himself. Our eventual solution was for the women to play partners together against the men. When we did, Bella and I often won because the men were so determined to win that they couldn't resist overbidding.

Another pastime was a little bit of gambling. Florida is no Las Vegas, but we became horse race fans. We read about turf and sulky racing, about pacers and trotters, about jockeys and stables, and mudders and purses and winning streaks and up or down in class. We learned that the trackman is not always right, handicappers are a dime a dozen, and to quit while you're ahead.

Then we discovered Jai-Alai (pronounced Hi-Li). We couldn't find a book that covered Jai-Alai so we learned through trial and error. The first thing I learned was that Jai-Alai was a game best watched through the cracks between my fingers clasped tightly over my eyes.

Unlike the races, a game of Jai-Alai isn't over with one quick lope around the track. Jai-Alai is played in a granite and marble court -- a fronton -- where one player serves a goatskin-covered ball called a pelota. It travels up to 150 mph against the front wall, for his opponent to receive in a curved basket called a cesta, strapped to his arm. He, in turn, hurls it on a return to the front wall. Games can last so long and be so exciting that the spectators are limp with exhaustion – sometimes more so than the players.

There is a teeth-on-edge tension. Nerves twang at the sharp thunk of the ball as it hits the cesta; the squeal of rubber soles as the player pivots, then leaps to reach the ball; the zing as it is hurled through the air to crack like a pistol shot against the granite slab wall and the cheers as a player leaps up the wall or into the side net to retrieve a shot.

The suspense when several players are neck-to-neck with 5 or 6 points each can't compare to the brief suspense of a horse or dog running the WIN mark.

Renaud liked having a system for placing bets. "We'll buy one ticket in the first game. To win," said Renaud. "Then, on the next, we'll buy 2 tickets on the same post position. To win. Then 3. Then if we win, we'll go back to betting only one again." Once, when we got to the 6th without any luck, I protested.

"Never mind," said Renaud. "We'll win yet."

"Yes," I said dryly, "If it takes every cent we have."

"We're OK," said Renaud.

"We are?" I asked

"Sure," he said. "The important thing to remember is not to panic."

"And then what?" I asked. "What if we get to the 8th or 10th game and still haven't won? Then what's the plan?"

"Ah...." he said. "*Then* we panic."

Romé and Bella usually came with us to Jai-Alai. Unless Linda was with us, then they stayed with her at the motel. Romé bet conservatively, and usually lost. Bella bet quenelles, casually, one game per outing. Then she dozed off through the rest of the games. Sometimes she won, sometimes she lost. She didn't care. She had the best system of all.

We weren't the only ones with a system. We certainly weren't the only losers. "I still like the one in the orange shirt," said the woman in front of us. "I'll bet on him again."

"It's not the same player every time," her partner said.

"Yes, it is. I bet on the orange shirt in the last game, and he has the same number on his sleeve every time."

"Yes, but they change shirts according to their new post position," he explained. "The post position is the number you see on the sleeve."

"I don't think so," she argued.

"Look," said her partner, "The one you liked in the last game is going to be in the blue shirt in this game."

"Are you sure about that?" she asked sharply.

"Yes, I'm sure," he said. "Look, the players' own numbers are on the backs of their shirts, and it says their names right here on the program."

"Well, I'm going to bet on the one in the orange shirt anyway. I like orange."

The players lined up on the court facing the spectators and saluted with raised cestas. The woman in front of us gaily raised her arm in a return salute, but by the 9th game, she wasn't saluting anymore and she and her partner weren't speaking to each other.

Another couple, betting modestly on each game, never came close to winning. Finally, at the end of one game the wife sprang to her feet. "I won!" she screamed, jumping up and down and banging her husband's arm.

"No you didn't," he said patiently. "Your man came in second."

"Yes, and I have a ticket on him."

"Your ticket is on him to win. He came in second."

"You mean that he came in, but I lost anyway?"

"That's right."

"I lost, eh?"

"Yes, you lost."

Jai-Alai, like the races, is a thrill – but not something to count on.

What's Cooking?

Bella and I did our best in the cooking department, but Vito's skimpily endowed kitchen shelves couldn't compare to the well-stocked cupboards and freezer at home. Since Renaud and Romé were not the sort to make do with a loaf of bread, a jug of wine and thou, even on vacation, Bella, Linda and I braced ourselves for the annual challenge.

Our Florida kitchenette was not equipped to turn out home-crafted meals. It measured 4½ feet by 5½ feet and contained, to the left of the doorway, a sink next to 1½ feet of counter space on one side and a short drain board on the other. On the small counter were toaster, teakettle and plastic tray containing a few knives, forks, spoons, and a spatula. There were half-filled salt-and pepper shakers and one unbelievably large, dull butcher knife for everything from pounding steak, to slicing ham and paring vegetables.

A vintage, 2-burner gas stove, and an ancient refrigerator that revved up noisily every 15 minutes, completed the picture.

The cupboard under the sink contained 2 pots, one too small and one too large, and an enormous at-least-3-pound cast-iron frying pan.

The one overhead cupboard held 4 big beer mugs (not great for morning orange juice or wine with dinner), 20 very large dinner plates, 5 soup bowls and no small plates, mixing bowls or storage containers.

Renaud and Romé checked out the kitchenette when we moved in and immediately declared it perfect. "You have everything you could possibly need here. Just like at home."

Bella and I looked at each other, making mental lists. We would manage somehow, but we were aware, even if they weren't that salt and pepper could only do so much.

Preparing food in Vito's kitchenette was not only challenging, it was haunted. Otherwise why would the cupboard door swing open for no reason, almost braining Bella when she stood up after bending over to pick up something.

There was also a wall-mounted can opener. Attached by a hinge, it stuck out in such a way that you could count on running into it on a regular basis. The toaster wouldn't let go of the toast without a fight, the refrigerator door wouldn't stay shut unless you pressed the upper right hand corner, and we tripped the circuit breaker or blew out the main fuse every time we plugged in the tea kettle and forgot that something else was also connected.

There were restaurant meals occasionally, but most of the meals were prepared in our little kitchenette. Because the standard kitchen staples were not on hand, meal planning and grocery shopping had to be managed accordingly. Here, we could not take for granted such ordinary things as bread, butter, coffee, sugar, cream, paper napkins, paper towels, detergent, soup, crackers, cheese, eggs, bacon, peanut butter, juice, ketchup, milk and fresh fruits and vegetables. Since we didn't want to overstock, leaving to go back north with cupboards full, we had to select what would constitute bare minimum to keep us operating.

While our men didn't participate in grocery shopping, meal planning or food preparation at home, we experienced a turnabout in Florida because they were on holiday and had time to participate. They said they wanted to help. A slight complication to this determination was the fact that on holiday they aspired to the untried. The exotic.

As I peered at rump roasts in the meat department of our local Winn Dixie, Renaud pressed against me, nudging me along toward the next aisle. "We eat roasts at home," he said. "Let's try something different."

"Like what?" I asked as the beautiful, lean roast faded in the distance.

"How about patte a cochon," he said.

"We have that at home too." I said.

"Or look, wow, there's octopus!"

From the moment we entered Winn Dixie or Publix, the men hung onto us like burrs. They felt it their duty to drag their feet at every purchase that didn't smack of the exotic, complaining when we womenfolk reached for something familiar. "Flour? You can't eat flour! What do you need flour for? You have flour back home. We're certainly not going to start buying supplies for a whole year down here."

"Cooking oil? You can't eat cooking oil! What do you need cooking oil for? You have cooking oil back home...." and on and on and on. They thought they were being helpful, but it looked suspiciously as though just because we had food in the cupboard back home in St. Anicet, we didn't need it here in Florida.

Strolling along the grocery aisles, Renaud and Romé browsed intently in the gourmet section. "Let's try these creamed toad's heels. And how about these marinated grasshopper noses..." And, "What wine goes good with smoked eel?"

Bella kept silent as the men made their recommendations, but their interpretation of nouvelle cuisine didn't sound like we could look forward to a vacation from the kitchen. Renaud dropped a can of kangaroo-tail soup into the shopping cart and he and Romé headed for the wine racks while Bella and I sidled over to vegetables, dairy products and soups, sending Linda to get jam, peanut butter, raisin bran cereal and milk.

With all the subterfuge, we forgot coffee. The next morning, the men gave us indignant looks because, "For goodness sake, we just bought groceries yesterday afternoon - and already you need more groceries? Can't you women get organized?" Well, not with the likes of them helping....

Then, there was the time I bought frozen chopped onions that looked exactly like frozen potatoes for hashbrowns, and didn't discover it until they were sizzling fragrantly with the bacon and eggs.

There was also the frozen pumpkin pie that was not only frozen, but raw, and we had to light the scary old gas oven so we could bake it.

But it really *was* my fault the time the canned spaghetti and meatballs were nicely heated and ready to serve and my sleeve caught on the handle of the heavy cast iron frying pan and propelled meatballs, tomato sauce and spaghetti into orbit around the little kitchenette sending everybody cowering.

For the worst vacation grocery disaster of all, I place the blame squarely upon the impatient men, who rushed us out of Winn Dixie before Bella and I had time to choose something for supper. As they jostled us toward the checkout, I hurriedly snatched a can of beef hash from a display island en route.

That evening, I opened the can of beef hash, dumped it into the frying pan and sniffed it, finding the odour not unfamiliar (it smelled vaguely like Alpo). Still, the can said beef hash, and there were these neat little cubes of potato, and slices of carrot, and yes, even some peas – must be OK

As it heated in the frying pan, even with onion added, and plenty of butter, salt and pepper, the Alpo aura hung pronouncedly in the air.

There were no complaints about the hash supper. Nor was there any enthusiasm, but on clearing the table and washing up, I glanced again at the empty can on the drain board, and there it was, in small print under the picture of a delicious looking plate of hash, 'For dogs'.

Well, there wasn't even a picture of a dog on the label for heaven's sake. Time for the industry to amend their packaging of pet foods. How was I supposed to know? I pushed the empty can deep into the garbage, crushed an egg carton on top of it, and kept my mouth shut. Anyway, nobody got sick. Kudos to the pet food industry - and they *have* since adjusted their labeling policy.

IV
GOING HOME

Fear of Shopping

Out of the grocery store, into the department store!

Shopping! Does anyone holiday without one shopping expedition?

Most men of our generation grew up with a prejudice against shopping.

Living in the countryside, as we did, distanced us from shopping venues. Renaud and I were busy with the business and raising a family; Bella and Romé were busy with family and the farming life. Romé farmed tobacco and hops. Tobacco farming was a big production involving ten tobacco kilns. The harvested leaves were strung on poles and hung in tiers in the kilns, where they were carefully tended, cured, bailed and then marketed.

Hops grew on twine strung high on poles. The whole family worked in planting the hop fields and harvesting. After the harvest and sorting along conveyer belts, the hops were dumped on screening midway up in the immense hop kiln. Then the blowers take over, tossing the hops in the air and drying them. These too had to be bailed and marketed.

Bella was equally busy. Besides caring for home, husband and children, she cared for her big kitchen garden and 100 hens - which produced egg money.

Needless to say, shopping was not a free-time recreational activity. There was *no* free time. When shopping had to be done, it was hurried, and mostly for farm essentials, school supplies, groceries, and to replace outgrown clothes.

Any wonder that with an opportunity like free time and Florida shopping centers, we women went off the deep end. Once a year.

Of course, the men didn't feel the same way about it. For instance, the only personal shopping Renaud ever did was in consideration of me. He wanted me to recognize that he remembered my birthdays, Christmas, Valentine's Day and our anniversaries. These shopping attempts were hurried and sometimes reflected an air of desperation, but he made the effort - and the heartfelt notes presented with those gifts told me what a very special man I had married.

Over the years I have been gifted with such items as an enormous kitchen carving knife, a goat-skin throw rug dyed crimson, three flocked plaster bluebirds, a set of screw drivers, two ceramic flower pots with donkeys for handles, a pair of pliers, a two-gallon can of paint, a laundry hamper, a big abandoned dog we named Happy, a can opener, an egg beater, another dog, named Rickey, a vice grip, a cat we called Putt-Putt, an aluminum step ladder, and a plastic orange tree.

Sometimes I also ended up with gifts of a more personal nature that included a purse, a gorgeous negligee, a compact and a set of dishes. While at least more gift-like, these efforts were destined to reflect the tastes of anyone Renaud could corner into doing his gift buying for him.

Now, I have a pretty good sense of humour, and I realize that it's possible to attach too much importance to the gifts men consider OK for giving. After all, it's the thought that counts. He remembered. He always did remember. I'm grateful for that. I'm one of those lucky women who, in spite of what the actual gift might be, knew for a fact that I had in this husband a true romantic. Never shy to show his affection, Renaud surrounded me with an ongoing aura of caring and tenderness. There was no coldness to his love. And although there were times when he was tense, worried, frustrated and exhausted by the business, he could still put his arms around me, could still take my hand and say "...don't worry, Mommy, we'll get past this." He could put his arms around me even across a crowded room with a wink, a smile and mouthing the words, "I love you."

These gestures did not take a great deal of planning or energy, but the thing is, he would do it - and the doing meant a lot. So what if he couldn't shop? He had better talents. He wrote little love notes on cards or paper bag scraps. He thought about *us*. The words on those notes will warm me for the rest of my days.

I often think back to the early days of our marriage, when we owned so little. When we married in 1952, we rented a small house and were lucky enough to buy its entire second-hand contents from the previous tenant, who joined the Merchant Navy and moved to Nova Scotia. The contents included half a raisin cake on a covered cake dish, salt and pepper in the shakers, and a wood stove in the kitchen.

Renaud arranged this while I was still in Greenland. I was one week back from Greenland when I saw it for the first time. A week later, upon returning from our New York City honeymoon, we moved in with our meagre cardboard boxes of personal possessions. We didn't have to buy a thing! Settling in, I discovered Renaud's box of souvenirs and mementos, which included a notebook full of gleanings: quotations, poems and observations, copied in his own hand. The reason this discovery had such an impact on me was that I had a similar collection. Many of the quotations we saved were identical, and the sentiments overall travelled parallel lines.

So when I look back at those gifts that ran the gamut of step ladders and pliers etc., I know that love has been represented on a daily basis through all the years of our marriage, and all the ceramic donkeys and plastic orange trees aren't saying, "...We can't afford it" or "We're cheapskates," what they're saying is, "I remembered!"

∞∞∞∞∞

The first time we vacationed in Florida - the year of the red tear-drop trailer - I initiated the habit of stowing little extras (sun-tan lotion, packs of cards, extra wash cloths, Band-Aids, aspirin, etc.) into the trunk of the car so we wouldn't have to shop for them while away.

In subsequent years, when the sky clouded over and rain threatened, we womenfolk tried to encourage a real shopping expedition. Renaud and Romé, however, didn't want to shop. "It's raining," they reasoned. "We can't go to the beach so let's go bowling!"

146

In the end, we nearly always ended up with one shopping trip, usually the last week of vacation. It became just one more of the travel games our men played.

Linda was 13 years old and travelling with us the year Bella and I decided to rattle their cages and insist on a real shopping expedition. There was still a week of holiday left. Bella wanted to buy a Florida dress. Something she had managed to do most years of our southern journeys. We told the men over supper that the next day we intended going to the big shopping mall in Palm Beach, about 5 miles down the road.

Renaud said, "In a couple of days, we'll be going home." He looked quizzically over at me to see how I was taking this observation, saw that it wasn't going too well, and added, "It's going to be a nice day for the beach." Romé pursed his lips. Nodding sagely he said, "Well, I certainly don't need anything."

Renaud added, "We'll be stopping at Service Centers all the way home. We can buy things there." And, looking hopefully at Bella, "Don't forget, it's winter back home."

We knew that, of course, but perversely I wanted to stamp my feet and shout something along the lines of "Why do you need a new bulldozer this spring - you already have a bulldozer?" But I knew it was no use because bulldozers help us earn a living, and souvenirs and summer dresses are unproductive.

Bella, Linda and I finally persuaded (they called it nagged) the men into taking us to the big shopping center, where they offered us a choice: 1. "We'll wait here. Don't

147

take more than 15 minutes." Or 2. "We'll come along and help."

We said we'd take the 15 minutes and go alone. Looking back furtively, we saw them following.

Bella, Linda and I deployed, thinking to edge the men toward the sports department, but they were too smart for us and split up, too. Romé followed Bella.

Gentle efforts to leave Renaud alone in the menswear department with the shopping cart were futile. "You know I'm no good at shopping," he said. "I need your help." As we cruised along, he picked up a summer shirt, slacks, socks, and a fishing lure. We headed for the checkout. Renaud took out his wallet and paid for his shopping.

Leaving Linda with our shopping cart of paid-for merchandise we went back to find Romé and Bella in the women's dress department. Romé waved cheerfully as we approached. While an exasperated Bella seemed to be having second thoughts about buying a dress, Romé was the one rummaging through the racks. He instantly found one that he liked, and urged Bella to try it on.

Bella, as any right-thinking woman, prefered to shop leisurely, without a husband who has a strong leaning to ribbons, bows, frills, lace, and low necklines.

"Here's a nice dress, Bella," Romé said, thrusting a frothy pink creation toward her.

"Oh, I can't wear a thing like that!" protested Bella.

Romé persisted. He believed that if you saw something on a hanger and liked it, you paid for it and that's that. Buying a dress isn't that simple. It should fit. Especially if you know that you won't be able to get back to exchange it. It should be comfortable. The style and colour should suit.

"I don't want a new dress now," Bella said, impatient with the whole business.

"Oh, yes, get a dress," said Romé. "Look, here's a pretty pale blue one. Buy this one."

The pretty blue dress had a swath of lace across the bodice, bugle beads around the shoulders (a real party dress) and was several sizes too large.

"I don't like that one," said Bella.

"But I want you to have a nice dress to take home from Florida. To show the children. A fancy dress. You know you want one."

"A nice dress takes *time*!"

"No, no, no, no, no.... *This* is a nice dress!" he said. "*This* is a *beautiful* dress."

"I don't like it."

"But you always get a Florida dress."

"Well, not this time."

"Aw, come on. The girls will expect it. They're all going to ask to see your new Florida dress."

"Well, I could use a house dress, I suppose." said Bella, reaching for a striped cotton. "How about this one?"

"But I don't *like* that one," said Romé. "It's too plain. It will make you look old."

"I *am* old," said Bella.

"Can't you get something young and bright?"

"No!" said Bella. "I don't want a dress now! I don't really need one anyway. Besides, you won't leave me alone to

149

choose what I want, and you don't like the style I like. It's no use. I can't shop with you around."

"Wait, look here," Romé persuaded eagerly. "Here's another nice dress. A yellow one, with all those shiny things all over it. If you want to try it on, I'll wait."

It was too little too late, but Bella looked at me helplessly. "What can I do?" she asked. "I don't want a dress any more. He's spoiled it for me. And now he wants me to buy a dress, but won't let me choose the style, the colour, the material, or even the size, for heaven's sake." It was all part of the games people play. Caza people, that is.

Homeward Bound

The mirrors in Vito's aging apartments were no better than those at old overnight motels en route. Maybe worse. The corrosive effect of salt air and humidity did nothing to promote an honest reflection. Still, however wavy, specked and tinted in greens, purples or yellows though they were, they were still clear enough for me to see that, by vacation's end, I was as pale as the day we arrived in Florida. As usual, this launched me into the annual last-minute campaign to return home with the southern vacationer's badge of a warm, golden tan.

There's no reasonable way to deal with a desire to return from vacation nicely tanned. Especially when that need is only perceived a couple of days before holiday's end.

We've never been sunbathers. Long hours stretched on the sand, frying in oil in the hot sun, was never our idea of fun. We would rather sit in the shade of a palm tree with a Walkman and a good book. That's why a sun tan was elusive - although it doesn't explain why it was sought after so persistently.

I remember the time I sat in the sun most of the day, two days before departure, itching with resentment because there were things I'd rather be doing. I wore my big new sunglasses, and while my skin took on quite a rosy glow by evening, next morning saw me sporting a brilliant burn-of-the-year, complimented by huge white circles around my eyes where the sunglasses protected. I looked like a raccoon, and felt like a boil.

I can't count the times I've gone contentedly pale throughout our vacation, only to spoil things by trying for the healthy look of a tan at the last minute, suffering throughout the return journey with peeling skin that did nothing for either looks or comfort. Not to mention a husband who dangled a headshake and an unsympathetic non-verbal "I told you so" glance at me whenever I winced.

Since Vito's place was close to Palm Beach and Riviera Beach, we often drove over to Singer Island, situated between the Atlantic Ocean and the Intracoastal Waterway. It was a lovely area even in those early days. We sometimes shopped at a small Winn Dixie there, which was adjacent to a drugstore. In was in that drugstore that I saw an advertisement that assured me my tanning problems were over. Science had developed a new product. A liquid tanning agent that guaranteed a painless tan overnight when smeared generously on the skin before retiring.

I bought 2 bottles of the stuff. One bottle might have been enough, but I was in a hurry. If one bottle was good, 2 should be twice as good. At least faster.

That night, after Renaud, Romé, Bella, and Linda went to bed, I tiptoed to the bathroom where I sloshed the clear, watery stuff lavishly over my arms, legs and face. No more time wasted lying in the sun; no more sunburns. Then I slid happily into bed, confident that in the morning a golden tan would be mine. It was guaranteed. It said so on the bottle.

In the morning, pleased to have saved time and put one over on Mother Nature, I bounded out of bed, rushed to the bathroom, looked in the mirror and recoiled in horror. Large and small rivulets, streams and splotches of orange-brown rampaged over my arms, legs and face. It was just as though I had been splashed generously with tobacco juice. And it wouldn't wash off! Not even with Ajax or Clorox.

The palms of my hands, which came in most frequent contact with the tanning liquid as I sloshed it around, were rust coloured. Today, such tanning products are tinted and creamy and so can be seen and evenly applied, but not then. In desperation, I put make-up over the splotches on my face. That evened things out a little, but also deepened my "tan."

That exotic colour, heightened by a furious blush, caused a few questioning stares at breakfast, a whoop of laughter from daughter Linda, and an amused smile and headshake from Renaud, who was used to me and, perhaps because of past experience, probably expected me to come up with something cock-eyed anyway.

∞∞∘∞

152

Another duty of the last week was getting rid of the bits and pieces of groceries on hand. Our final meals at the motel were leftovers, with mild complaints about no butter or sugar.

The early stage of packing the car involved pushing those things we thought we wouldn't need into far corners of the car trunk, and digging them out again when we discovered we needed them after all. It was also time to throw out smelly shellfish that Linda unknowingly packed while they were alive (they were dead enough by discovery though. And smelly enough, too).

The last stage proved that no matter how little shopping we did, or how good our intentions, there was too much stuff to fit into the car.

There were bags of coloured stones, a big conch shell, a giant starfish from Key West, a coconut with husk that Linda wanted to take to her brothers, and a dozen bottles of coconut spread Renaud bought for the men at work.

Eventually everything was wedged in and it was time for a last check through the apartment, under the beds, into closets and drawers, and the clothesline on the back patio.

It was time to go. We waved good-bye to Vito and our winter friends, took a last look at the sparkling waves slapping the sandy beach, and drove west to catch I-95 north. At least now, the southern sun shone in the back window and not in our eyes as it did on the way south. Homeward bound!

When an Ending is Just a Beginning

Heading north, we carried with us a pocketful of good memories and a funny suntan for me. We headed back to reuniting with the boys, collecting dog, cat and hamster. Back to work for Renaud, back to school for Linda and a plethora of Florida stories for Romé and Bella to tell their friends at the next Golden Agers' meeting.

The first day of the long drive north produced a kaleidoscope of palms, orange groves, fringes of Spanish moss and endless blue-grey highway.

Then the usual motel mixture, restaurant stops, a gas game or two and mild, somehow pleasant, arguments in the back seat.

Renaud's target for the first day on the road was to get across the Florida-Georgia border without a shopping, gas or vehicle crisis. But there was no escaping the obstacle course of souvenir shops and produce stands where his passengers wanted to pick up Claxton Fruit Cakes, pecan rolls, orange blossom honey etc. for family and friends. And so, the *Return from Florida* games began, with Renaud resolutely insisting that we couldn't cram anything else into the car.

He said, "How are we supposed to reach the spare tire if we get a flat, eh? Just tell me that. We'd have to empty the whole trunk on the side of the road and it might be raining! Did you think of that?" And, a happy afterthought, "...or snowing."

It all made sense, but Romé wasn't going to give up easily. He wanted to bring home oranges. There's no contest like pitting Caza against Caza. Romé had just been where oranges grow in winter, and by God, he was going to take some back to St. Anicet to prove it.

Finally on the road. The game started slowly as we covered the Florida miles. At first, Romé pretended that he hoped Renaud would stop on his own accord at a fruit stand before we got on the I-95, which was always under construction, leaving gaps throughout fruit-stand country.

After half an hour of zooming past such fruit stands, Romé launched his campaign in earnest. Clearing his throat, he leaned forward in his seat. "Renaud," he said solemnly as we drove toward a nest of open market stands full of fresh citrus. "Here's a good place."

"A good place for what, Pa?" asked Renaud.

"Well, just look at all those nice oranges!" said Romé "Just look at them! Hey! Slow down. Look at the prices, too. They're not expensive. Hey, you're passing them."

"What do you want oranges for, Pa?" asked Renaud. "You've had oranges all month."

"I know, I know," said Romé. "But don't you think it would be a good idea to buy a few to eat on the way?"

"We got a late start this morning," said Renaud. "If we keep stopping, we'll never make it to Georgia today."

"Aw, you know that it won't take five minutes to stop and buy a few oranges," said Romé.

"Oh ,sure, stop for oranges now, then stop for gas, then stop for a meal, then stop for rest rooms...." complained Renaud, stalling for time. "How far do you think we'll get today at that rate?"

"How long can it take to stop the car and buy a bag of oranges?" muttered Romé. "Why, they're so close we wouldn't even have to get out of the car."

"Maybe later, Pa," said Renaud. "If we make good time now."

"Humph!" grunted Romé. "By then we'll be on I-95 and there won't *be* any fruit stands!"

"There'll be plenty more before that Pa," said Renaud. Reflecting on past performance, it was clear, at least to me, that although he was stringing out the game he would eventually cave in and stop. Romé persisted.

"Aw ... Hey! Here's another one coming up on the right. Come on Renaud, stop the car."

Renaud shook his head. "Pa..."

"Oh, Oh! Look at that! Mes chers amis, Renaud - look at those beautiful oranges."

"Pa... You know!"

As we rolled along, the campaign gained intensity.

"Look, that sign says they're giving away free glasses of fresh-squeezed orange juice," Romé declared. "You know - come to think of it, I *am* thirsty. How about you, Linda - aren't you thirsty, too?"

"Oh sure," said Linda, getting into the spirit of things.

"So am I," said Bella, who wanted to buy little souvenirs for the children, grandchildren, friends and neighbours at home. She reminded Renaud that earlier, in the shopping center department store, the men had promised that we would stop en route for souvenirs.

Renaud said, "Pa, there's no room for bags of oranges. The trunk is full, and besides you can buy oranges right at home. In St. Anicet at Robidoux's or Chretien's. Or in Cazaville. So why buy them here and haul them all the way back with us?"

"That's not the same as oranges really from Florida. Picked ripe...," argued Romé. "And look here, we can put them right by my feet. They won't take up much room."

"Pa...."

"How about a bag of tangerines then, Renaud, a small one - to eat on the way."

"Pa...." Renaud knew it wouldn't stop with tangerines. It would be, "Let's throw in a couple of grapefruit, they're so lovely and sweet, and a bag of pecans and maybe a couple of those giant lemons like Bella noticed earlier."

Renaud was weakening so I wasn't surprised when he pulled off the road at one of the stands. Despite idle suggestions about being able to shop from the car window, everyone piled out to fritter away a whole 15 minutes while Renaud looked at his watch, then shifted suitcases around in the trunk to make space to stow bags of citrus and, although he complained bitterly, he certainly ate his share.

The following day, I was already braced for another special road game reserved for the return journey, and I'm sure Renaud was, too. We saw the first announcements mid-afternoon in the Carolinas. "No tax, Cigarettes! Special low, low prices! All brands! No limit!"

As the first small signs flittered by, Renaud looked nervously in the rear view mirror to see if Romé had seen them. Soon, there were bigger signs. Romé was wide awake now and taking notice. So was Bella, who said "Uh-oh," and nudged Linda. Linda tapped my shoulder and winked.

Renaud glanced back and shook his head in dismay as he saw Romé sit up straighter, his eyes following the cigarette announcements as they whooshed by.

Linda giggled in my ear, Bella looked at Romé, and her lips firmed in a tight line. I looked at Renaud. He was beaten before he started, and we were about to be entertained again.

"Uuuuuhhhh, Renaud," Romé said, after we swept past a particularly beguiling sign that promised 'low, low, LOW PRICES!' a few miles ahead. "I didn't buy cartons of cigarettes to bring home. Remember? You said we would get a better deal on the way back. Would you mind stopping at one of these places so I can get a carton or two?"

"Pa...."

"Aw, Renaud," he pleaded. "It won't take but a couple of minutes. And they're right here!"

"Pa...."

"Are you two going to go through all this again?" Bella exclaimed incredulously.

"Hummmm," I acknowledged, nodding. There was no doubt in *my* mind.

"Oh, Renaud, you *have* to stop!" Romé exclaimed. "Look, just look at those prices. Mes chers amis – do you realize how much cigarettes cost at home?!"

"Why don't you quit smoking, Romé? Then they won't cost anything," offered Bella sagely.

"Aw, Renaud...."

"Pa," said Renaud. "If you think I'm going to risk having an accident, taking the ditch, or crashing into a hydro pole just so you can buy cheap cigarettes...."

"But Renaud, the prices!"

"That's it, Romé, smoke!" said Bella.

"Pa...." said Renaud. "Those aren't bargains. They're cheap brands you've never heard of. They're no good."

"No, no, no." protested Romé. "I saw the signs. They said all brands. Look, there's another one! See!"

"We'll have to go through Customs before we get home, Pa." said Renaud.

"I'm allowed a carton," Romé said indignantly.

"You like filters, Pa. They just have plain ones."

"No, no, no - c'est pas vrai. That sign said both regular and filter," said Romé.

"Pa....."

"That's it, Romé. Smoke. Smoke!" said Bella.

Renaud finally gave in of course, and swerved off the highway, into the parking lot of a place with a big advertisement. Romé got out of the car, smiled, stretched, and said, somewhat defensively, "There, now that wasn't so much trouble now, was it?" Then grumbled that earlier we passed a gas station with an even better price deal.

Renaud said, "If you think I'm going to turn around and drive back there...."

Then Romé asked Renaud to accompany him inside to translate for him, which touched off another argument.

"You wanted to stop," said Renaud.

"Yes, but my English isn't too good," said Romé.

"Well, it was pretty good when you were reading the advertisements," grumbled Renaud getting out of the car and following his father into the building.

With all that, there was still time for another gas game before dark.

At the last motel stop before reaching home, there was snow. Renaud dragged the oranges into our room so they wouldn't freeze. Then Romé, arms full of overnight bags, walked full tilt into a long glass panel next to the closed door, that looked like an open doorway, and nearly knocked himself out.

After freshening up from our long day on the road, we settled in for a pre-supper gin and tonic and mild discussion of Caza ancestors.

After supper, at a within-walking-distance-of-our-motel restaurant, we settled into our room, lounging around, taking turns at the bathroom and getting ready for bed. We were feeling the quiet letdown of vacation's end. Tomorrow, we would be home. Two months of winter still ahead.

The next morning we had an early start and by suppertime crossed the border into Canada. We left Romé and Bella at their home. Fifteen minutes later we stood in our own living room.

After one month away, it was strange to step over the threshold and look around our small home that now looked big, after 5 people in crowded motel rooms for a month.

I took a mental glimpse backward, to when we hurried to the car to start our holiday. A jumbled rush and instant replay of the month condensed into seconds. Everything here was exactly as we had left it.

Our dirty breakfast dishes sat in the sink with one-month-old dried-on egg, left unwashed because by the time I had cleared the table, Renaud had shut off the water and was under the house draining the pipes.

Dried mud decorated the floor too, from that pipe work, because there had been no water left to mop up the mess. Come to think of it, I had even set out that day with my face unwashed.

Now to get into the work lane again. Back to getting up at 6:00 a.m., readying the kids for school and Renaud for work. Back to winter boots and snow-caked snowsuits and a stack of month-old letters and bills. Back to the familiar sag of bed and sofa, and windows shrouded in snow.

But first things first. Time to prepare a quick shopping list and head to the village store. After I checked the fridge and discarded a half bottle of lumpy old milk, a bowl of red Jell-O, dried up and shrunken and other dried up bits and pieces, I turned a questioning look to Renaud. "What do we need?" Eggs, milk, butter, bread, vegetables, coffee, cheese, meat, cereal. Memory would not suffice. "Linda, see if you can find a pencil and paper."

As she scurried off, Renaud and I looked at each other. He put his arm around my shoulder and gave me a brief hug, saying, "Well, Mommy, we're back home. I'll get the water turned on, you turn up the heaters, and then we'll stop at the store and go pick up the boys. The honeymoon is over -- but wait 'til next year," he grinned.

EPILOGUE

By 1976, we wondered if we would ever get out of the rut of our haphazard, unpredictable travels. That was the year we visited friends from St. Anicet who wintered in a Ft. Lauderdale mobile home park. This introduced us to a more anchored aspect of Florida living. The following year, Renaud's brother Yves and his family bought a mobile home in that same park.

In 1979, we spent a week in Yves' mobile home before going back to Vito's and, while strolling through the park streets the last evening before vacation's end, we saw a FOR SALE sign on a beautiful mobile home. A big one. 24 ft. x 74 ft. Far from the memories of the short red trailer in 1953.

We paused in our walk, admiring the property: It had a tangerine tree, full of blossoms and fruit. There was a big, screened Florida Room, a curved concrete driveway, a mailbox and a brass door knocker. It was beautiful!

The lady of the house opened the door at that point, saw us admiring her home, and invited us in. We were given the grand tour: Christmas tree in the living room, fireplace, huge kitchen with center island and four wheeled leather kitchen chairs. A dining room, family room, separate laundry area. A front door, a back door and a side door! A separate wet bar adjacent to the Florida Room. There was a big master bedroom with en-suite bathroom. Even the guest room had its own bathroom.

It was lovely. But could we afford it? Maybe. We'd worked hard, and business was good. However, it would not be worth owning a place in Florida if we continued only taking one-month holidays. Could we get away for 3 or 4 winter months? We said goodbye to the owners, told them we were leaving the next morning, but would think about buying the mobile home. We would call them.

Back home the vision of extended holidays and our very own home in Florida faded with the pressures of business and family life.

Then, a phone call. The owners of the mobile home had an offer. We made an offer. This went back and forth for three days and finally agreement was reached. We flew to Ft. Lauderdale mid-January and bought the mobile home.

∞∞∞∞

During all this melee of shoehorn in holidays and escaping winter, the family grew older and, although each of the children have been on holiday with us at one time or another, they too, soon settled into their own lives.

In retrospect, I found it incredible that, with all our packing problems, our daughter, Linda, grew to maturity with sensible suitcase genes, could pick up at a moment's notice, without fuss or fanfare and travel light. Like the year when she and Roland, her American Vietnam War Veteran husband returned to that country. They travelled to 9 areas during their 2-week visit. During preparation for this journey, I asked her if she needed any suitcases to take along on their journey and was humbled at her response that they had all they needed. One carry-on each. They have been volunteers in South East Asia for 10 years now, and have 5 children and 7 grandchildren, scattered throughout Canada and the United States. And they still travel light and easy.

Joey developed skills as a cook and worked at hospitals and a detention center. He bought a farmette nearby, and has taken to buying antiques and refinishing furniture.

Bill settled into our construction business, but not before spreading his wings to the Fort McMurray oil sands as a machine operator (here he and a friend were mugged upon leaving a bank after cashing their first pay cheques). Then there was a stint in Morocco, instructing on operation and maintenance of construction equipment. He married Suzanne in the company gravel and sand pit in a magnificent mid-summer tented ceremony and their reception included barbeque, swimming and beach activities.

As for us, the golden years brought more travels for Renaud and me. Cruises, seniors' group tours, and Elderhostel (including hosting an Ederhostel program in St. Anicet).

There were also the to-be-expected realities of aging, of course, but, ah, it was, and continues to be, a life well lived.

ABOUT THE AUTHOR

Born in Fredericton, New Brunswick in 1930, Margaret Crawford, at the tender age of one, moved with her family to Campbellton, New Brunswick, on the shores of the Restigouche River. In 1948 they again pulled up roots and moved to the Province of Quebec, where she graduated from business college. Two jobs later she worked in Greenland with the U.S. Air Force, returning home in 1952 to marry her French Canadian engineer fiancé, Renaud Caza. Cascading life events provided fodder for her first book, *Walk Alone Together*, nominated for the Stephen Leacock award for humour. Next she produced *The Lights of Lancaster*, the diary of a family-member stroke victim. *Just One Suitcase?!* is her third book. Margaret, who lost Renaud, her beloved life partner, to cancer in 1990, is currently working on a retirement article series, "The Sunny Side of the Street."